Man of the Southern: Jim Evans Looks Back

'Steam Past' Books from Allen & Unwin

THE LIMITED by O. S. Nock
THE BIRTH OF BRITISH RAIL by Michael R. Bonavia
STEAM'S INDIAN SUMMER by George Heiron & Eric Treacy
GRAVEYARD OF STEAM by Brian Handley
PRESERVED STEAM IN BRITAIN by Patrick B. Whitehouse
TRAVELLING BY TRAIN IN THE EDWARDIAN AGE by Philip Unwin
MEN OF THE GREAT WESTERN by Peter Grafton
MAN OF THE SOUTHERN: JIM EVANS LOOKS BACK by Jim Evans
MAUNSELL'S NELSONS by D. W. Winkworth

STEAM YEAR BOOK edited by Roger Crombleholme and Terry Kirtland

Man of the Southern: Jim Evans Looks Back

Jim Evans
Edited by Peter Grafton

London
GEORGE ALLEN & UNWIN
Boston   Sydney

First published in 1980

GEORGE ALLEN & UNWIN LTD
40 Museum Street, London WC1A 1LU

©   Jim Evans and Peter Grafton, 1980

*This book was compiled from a series of articles written for the Merchant
Navy Locomotive Preservation Society Magazine.*

British Library Cataloguing in Publication Data
Evans, Jim
Man of the Southern.
1. Locomotives – England
2. Southern Railway (Great Britain)
I. Title   II. Grafton, Peter
385′.092′4   TJ603.4.G72S67   80–40106

ISBN 0–04–385078–2

Picture research by Mike Esau

Book designed by Diane Sawyer/Design Matters

Typeset by Inforum Ltd, Portsmouth
Printed and bound in Great Britain
by Biddles Ltd Guildford, Surrey

Contents

Illustrations

1
The Early Years

Let's start at the beginning. Having had a grandfather and three uncles on the footplate, it was a matter of course that I would become the third generation of what was, in my opinion, the most glamorous and rewarding occupation ever.

As a boy, engine spotting was not for me. *I* could sit around the table with a main line driver and three firemen, and listen to footplate arguments and experiences that all footplate men enjoyed so much. Second regulator, valve cutoff, rough trips, prickers and darts were all old hat to me long before I left school.

Grandfather started his railway career as a cleaner at Basingstoke in 1895, eventually becoming a fireman at Nine Elms. Over 130 tank engines were shedded there to cover suburban work, and the main line men worked to Dorchester. It was then a recognised thing for firemen to come to work in their spare time to clean the tubes and tube plate before starting duty. As crews had their own engines, it paid dividends to look after them. The driver was paid a percentage of the price of the coal he saved and this was the reason why clean tubes and tube plates were essential. The better the engine steamed, the less coal would be consumed and so the bigger the driver's bonus at the end of the month. If he was in a good mood, perhaps he would reward his fireman with a shilling for his trouble.

On leaving school at the age of 14, I presented myself at Bournemouth Motive Power Depot, but Mr Collins, the shedmaster, said that he couldn't employ me until I was 15. He suggested that I should find a job in the Traffic Department and come back in a year's time.

Thus I found myself as a booking-boy in Bournemouth Central signal box. What a wonderful vantage point this was for watching the comings and goings of the steam engines to and from the depot. The Dorchester men worked up from Weymouth with their T9s, there were the Brighton men with their Atlantics, the Midland men who worked the old Somerset and Dorset line with their Black 4s and 5s, and many others that are now only a memory. At that time, the main line engines at Bournemouth were the Schools. Eastleigh crews were blessed with the Nelsons and, although the Nine Elms men performed with a variety of locomotives, their principal engine was the very versatile King Arthur. The Merchant Navy class was still to come to Bournemouth.

Eventually, however, the time came for me to apply for employment in the MPD. An application for a transfer was submitted to the station

1. King Arthur class no. 789, 'Sir Guy', a simple, straightforward engine, no frills or gimmicks but capable of performing any job. At the time of this 1947 photo 789, along with 787 and 790, had just been transferred to Bournemouth from the West Country. So good were these engines that the late Driver Jack Atfield of Bournemouth had 790 as his regular engine on the main line in preference to a Lord Nelson. This would explain why Jack always wore immaculate overalls: he had no inside motion to oil. All his oiling was confined to the outside. Note the snifting valve on the smokebox (there was also one on the other side). These were to vent the superheater tubes to prevent them burning when steam was shut off, because only when the regulator was open did the superheater tubes have any steam in them. As the regulator was opened the passage of steam through the header and tubes would close these valves when under pressure, denoted by a short puff of steam from each valve. Shortly after nationalisation in 1948 snifting valves were removed from all the superheated engines on the Southern. Whether it was because the tubes were then made of a different metal remains to be found out. Or did Mr Bulleid, then the Southern Chief Mechanical Engineer, have other ideas?

master, and mislaid in true railway tradition. Many words of advice went in one ear and out of the other on the advantages of being a signalman. No, thank you: I wanted the footplate. 'But think of all the dirt, the smell, the heat and work. A signalman's lot is clean and dry.' No thanks! I was going to be a top link driver.

On 22 October 1945, I again presented myself at the shedmaster's office. Mr Collins peered at me over his glasses, in disgust I thought, but I learned later that he was measuring me up against a notch cut in the door-post, the notch being at the minimum height for cleaners. After reading numerous notices to me concerning my future employment, he sent me off to the foreman cleaner, Tom Glassey.

Men old enough to be my father were cleaners under Tom. *He* knew every trick that cleaners knew to evade work, all the hiding places that

could be used for a game of cards. We tried to beat him, but Tom was unbeatable. He was chasing young cleaners to work long before I was born. His often-used phrase, 'C'mon let's 'ave yer', would send oily little boys scurrying back to their engines, but many threats of 'I'll take yer up the top door, my lad' were never carried out. The foreman cleaner is yet another one of the many 'behind the scenes' jobs that has disappeared with the advent of modernisation, and the like of which we shall never see again.

Having been issued with a set of second-hand overalls, I was shown by Tom how to spread crude paraffin on the engines to loosen dirt, and how to wipe it off. Believe it or not, this left quite a good shine. We boys worked in gangs of five: two on the boiler, two on the tender with one for the underneath and side rods. The latter task was generally given to the youngest boy on the gang.

Any cleaner over the age of 16 could be used for firing duties, in strict order of seniority, but because I was only 15 I could not be booked out. However, many times the running foreman

2. Drummond goods and express engines. 700 class no. 30317, with six driving wheels, was an engine designed for goods work. Providing they had a good head of steam they would pull anything. For some reason they were not fitted with a steam-heat pipe to the front. Additional lugs fitted to the lower part of the smokebox door prevented air being drawn in through the ashes which would cause combustion inside the smokebox and burn the door. Fitting of these lugs did not appear to be a uniform practice, and was not confined solely to these engines. Here, on 18 July 1953, 30317 is being worked back to her home depot of Salisbury, as pilot to T9 no. 30721, having spent the day working between Poole, Hamworthy and Wimborne. Piloting a regular passenger train was convenient with the tablet working over the single line.

would be short of a fireman and having only me in cleaning, would send me out. As long as he could scrape up somebody to get the engine in service it didn't matter how old he was and for quite some time I was, literally, 'the bottom of the barrel'! Then would come the meeting with the driver as I hauled my full five feet three up on to the footplate.

'What do *you* want?'

'I've got to come with you, mate.'

11

'Who said so?'

'The foreman, mate.'

'How old are you?'

'Fifteen, mate.'

'Been out firing before?'

'A few times, mate.'

'Huh! Trust me to get a dud fireman and engine!'

At that time, we didn't go to school to learn how to fire an engine, so we were instructed by the drivers. This was resented by some for they had an image to live up to although, as I pointed out, *they* had had to learn once. This was the way we learned how to use a shovel, prepare and dispose an engine and control the boiler in service: much criticism, a lot of mistakes and no praise.

As soon as a cleaner was rostered to his first firing turn, he was issued with a cap and black serge jacket. His turns were carefully noted and counted, for when he had performed 313 turns he was issued with his Southern Railway Engineman's badge. This was indeed as big step in the right direction, for now we started to look like enginemen. Even now, many men wouldn't

3. No. 30111 dropping down the bank into Swanage. The 17.02 from Bournemouth was another Bournemouth duty, an extra push-pull coach being added for the increased passenger traffic. The fireman has put on the disc board ready for the return trip to Wareham; this practice was frowned on at one time but in later years the fireman would get away with it. 30111 had a very good name, being quite fast and free-steaming, and her regular crew kept the boiler front polished and painted. My driver saw little point in this, and on the rare occasions that this engine came our way he would lose no time in telling me that it was like working in a so-and-so fairground.

4. Tightening the smokebox door of West Country no. 34023, 'Blackmore Vale', at Waterloo. This should have been done before leaving Nine Elms, and that front framing should have been swept off. When I used to prepare engines at Bournemouth we dared not leave one speck of smokebox ash on the front framings — at speed it would blow back into the driver's face and was very dangerous. There was no generator on this engine, hence the use of paraffin lamps. But what happened to all the Southern lamps? These LMS lamps were not as efficient as our SR lamps. The plate the fireman is standing on covers the mechanical lubricators — not a very good design as it was impossible to keep the mechanism of the lubricators free of ashes.

3. Mike Esau

part with that badge. To me, mine is priceless.

Becoming registered as a permanent fireman was a formality. Vacancies for firemen would be advertised and the senior cleaners filled the jobs. After a medical and eyesight test, that was it. Cleaning days were over and one was now a fireman placed on the roster with a regular driver, trying to mould one's work to his liking.

My career as a fireman began with me rostered in the lowest link – the Bournemouth yard shunter, with regular engine Adams tank no. 260. My driver was a man nearing retirement who treated every shunt movement as a main line trip. Looking back, perhaps he had the right idea. Whenever the engine was on the move I had to be on my feet keeping a sharp look-out. If

5. No. 30171, known as a 'Big Hopper'. This was a saturated engine as opposed to the superheated T9, with smaller driving wheels and lower splashers. Considering the age of this locomotive the lack of steam blows is remarkable. There is just a slight blow from the steam reverser showing under the front bogies. She has also been in a collision at one time, to judge by the state of the front offside buffer. Being provided with a good-sized tender for coal and water, these engines were capable of anything short of express running on the Southern. In this picture 30171 is seen at Eastleigh with a stopping train to Brockenhurst on 14 July 1951. She was withdrawn the following September.

I put coal on the fire and made smoke, he would hurl abuse at me. If the engine blew steam through the safety valves, again I would be treated to a run-down on the uselessness of the modern generation, sprinkled with many adjec-

14

tives, and told that I would never make a fireman as long as I had a hole in my ear. If I let the tank run over when taking water, I would be assured in no uncertain terms that all the oil would be washed out of the boxes and she would run hot. Strangely enough, she never did. This old driver was treating me as he was treated when he was a young fireman, possibly at the turn of the century.

Often, when I was on night shift in this link, a young cleaner would be put in my place and I would be sent on loan to Salisbury. This entailed catching the up Mail to Eastleigh and then the West of England Mail across to Salisbury. Both of these trains were worked by T9s – truly Drummond's best engines. On arrival, I collected a Salisbury driver and worked the 4 am goods to Bournemouth, the engine being a Black Motor of the 690 breed. Now I really was progressing, for after going up and down Bournemouth yard eight hours a day, this seemed like Glasgow and back. The route was over the old Fordingbridge and Wimborne road, more often than not with full loads of sixty-five wagons. I didn't get much time to view the countryside, because my lack of experience was making the job harder than it really was.

As tablet changing had to be executed at speed, this was done by the driver, with a curt 'I'll have it'. Here was something else I learnt – the right way to exchange single line tablets on the move. The names on the tablet were read out aloud to the driver, to ensure we had the correct one.

One night I fell asleep in the West of England train and woke up at Templecombe, a place I didn't know existed. The signalman stopped a passing train and I hitched a lift back to Salisbury. Having missed my turn, I caught the next train back to Bournemouth without telling anyone. On arriving home I was told by my mother that Mr Collins had been in touch with her to say

that I had signed on and they had lost me. She promptly sent me back to work, where Mr Collins gave me a telling off with a smile on his face, and a fatherly talk about making sure I had enough sleep – off duty.

The next step up from yard shunter was the 'Poole Bug' gang where I spent six weeks working on the B4s. I would fill up the firebox of our engine with lumps straight from the coal wagons, and as there was little, if any, brick arch and a door nearly as wide as the box itself, quite a lot could be crammed in. As a result, this would normally last for a full shift. We had a regular engine which was no. 93 and my driver, even though well over sixty, treated me as a mate, regardless of the difference in our ages. Co-operating together in keeping the engine and brasswork clean made going to work a pleasure.

The next roster was allocation to the preparation and disposal gang. As we were the lowest complete gang on the roster with junior firemen and drivers, all the menial turns came our way. You really started to earn your money now with early turns, mostly preparing engines, and late turns, disposing of them. My mate this time was a much younger man, just appointed as a driver at Bournemouth. We got on very well together, perhaps helped by the fact that he used to fire to my grandfather.

On the late turns, we would relieve the crews, berth the trains and dispose of the engines. Three engines were relieved in the course of a duty, either Schools, Arthurs or Nelsons. How we young firemen hated those Nelsons. Open the smokebox and jump clear! If the driver who'd worked the train down had been a bit heavy-handed, the smokebox ash would be red hot, and by the time you had emptied the smokebox and swept the ashes of the front, the fire would nearly be out. (Having the smokebox door open for so long with the dampers shut caused the

firebox to lose its heat, and the fire to be reduced to burnt ashes.) This meant making some fire before you could start to clean out the clinker, otherwise, by the time this had been done, there wouldn't be enough fire left to save; then you would be chasing round looking for sleepers or any old wood to re-light it.

If pieces of stone had been placed on the firebars, the clinker would lift out easily, but more often than not it had to be chipped off piece by piece. As drop grates were not fitted every-

6. Pushing out of Brockenhurst to Lymington in September 1960, again with an extra coach, this one in the afternoon for the children going home from school. Note the provision for electric lights on the front of the coach, though I have never seen these fitted. This was a Lymington turn of duty, as there was a depot then at Lymington. Lymington men worked up and down this line all day, being relieved for one trip per shift by Bournemouth men to enable them to perform engine requirements. Like the drivers and firemen at Swanage, Lymington men were quite content in their little world away from the main line, but while there was a lot in favour of this sort of work it would not have suited me.

16

thing had to be shovelled out on the end of a clinker shovel. This was really hard work. Nothing was worse than to get a good shovelful of clinker balanced just right, pull it towards the fire door with a cloth in each hand smoking with the heat of the shovel and your palms getting hotter, go to lift it over the end of the fire door and everything drops off. You just had to dig it out from under the door and start again.

After cleaning the fire and putting on enough coal to keep it alight, you would then have to hunt for the ashpan rake to perform this part of the disposal duties. The Nelsons had two ash-pans, one above the other. The top pan could only be raked out from the back as it was right above the trailing driving axle, and if the wind was blowing in the wrong direction raking out

was most unpleasant. Nelsons numbered 860 upwards had a form of drop grate, a trapdoor in the grate two-thirds down the box, but as they were inclined to stick they were rarely used.

What a wonderful sight in those days, though. A pit road full of engines of all classes gently

7. M7 no. 30053, now relegated to sentry duty inside the gate at Steam Town in the USA. If any class paid back its cost of building these Motor Tanks did. They seemed to go on for ever. This photo was taken after the withdrawal of the push-pull stock, the engine having to run round at Brockenhurst and Lymington Pier. Notice how the coach dwarfs the engine, also the AWS box below the rear framing and this time no lugs on the smokebox door. There are the first signs of officialdom taking over from experience, the names of the pipes being painted on the front buffer beam. As a point of interest one Drummond, no. 126, tank was fitted out as a superheated.

7. G. R. Siviour

weeping steam after the day's work. Cascades of red-hot clinker and fire lighting up the engines with a red glow; red hot fire irons flashing in and out, the flare lamps of the driver looking round his charge, the piles of clinker crackling and turning to blue hues before dying out. Much as we disliked disposal duties, this was a sight to stir the heart of any engineman.

So we came to 1948 and the nationalisation of the railways. During the year I moved up a link into the senior goods – much the same work as the junior, but with fewer shunting duties. My driver was an ex-Brighton man and a firm believer in the use of the blower for making steam. He used to say, 'It's there, and if you want to use it, use it!' Why *did* the old Bournemouth

drivers object to the use of the blower? They would let it be used when preparing the fire and to prevent back-draught at the fire door, but otherwise it might as well not have been there. With some of the men this even applied to the pricker. If there were difficulties in maintaining

8. Another 700 class: 'Black Motor' no. 30690 on a regular Bournemouth turn, shunting at Ringwood in 1956. The flat area behind the ground frame was used as a prisoner-of-war camp during the 1914–18 war, the close proximity of the railway being an advantage. The line leading off to the left of the berthed passenger stock used to lead to a turntable. Drivers have told me of the engine shed and table that used to be there. This was in fact not a motive power depot but the berthing point for an engineer's engine, dating back to when engineers were building railways instead of destroying them, and each with his personal engine.

9. R. A. Panting

steam pressure they would tell you in no uncertain terms that 'the shovel is to make steam with and not the blower or pricker'.

Nelsons, Schools and Arthurs were still the main line engines at Bournemouth. The Bulldogs, big and small Hoppers, Paddleboats and Double Breasters were disappearing to be broken up, but their going was not noticed to any extent. I've always felt that this can be likened to the retiring of a driver. He walks out of the gate for the last time after forty-five to fifty years, and nobody seems to miss him; the only concern is for the shift up through the links.

By now I had learnt, and was trying to carry

9. B4 class no. 30093 shunting on Poole Quay in July 1959. This was a regular trip twice a day, taking the oil, coal and grain through the streets of Poole to be loaded on to the boats in the morning and returning in the evening to pick up the empties. Note the man standing beside the engine; he walked in front with a red flag, visible behind his back, and at night he would carry a red lamp. Often on the slow journey through Poole the crew would be called upon to help lift a parked car clear of the line. Just behind the safety valves can be seen the original round 'spy glass', so typical of Southern engines. This engine was built with an open-sided cab with the crew exposed to the elements. When the sides were covered over it was much cheaper to install square windows in a wood frame. These engines were braked by hand, although it was possible to work a vacuum train, a vacuum ejector and pipes being fitted.

19

out, the finer arts of firing. No two engines were the same and no two drivers treated an engine in the same way. I could bounce coal off the front of a Nelson's box without hitting the brick arch and, if I had small coal, could fire to an engine over the top of the half-door – a gap of about four inches. I knew how to adjust an injector to maintain a constant water level in the boiler, equalising the amount being used by the driver. On long, non-stop runs, this was essential, as the water that would be wasted by constant use of the injector could add up to quite a few gallons – remember, on the Southern there were no water troughs every few miles to enable the fireman to fill up the tender, so correct use of the injector was important.

When an engine was in good condition the job was relatively easy: fire little and often; sweep the footplate and dampen down; keep the coal trimmed and damp to eliminate dust; and make sure that you see every distant signal. It was

10. M7 no. 30057, my regular engine with driver Frank Tizzard when in the push-pull gang at Bournemouth. This 1960 shot shows clearly the push-pull equipment, the Westinghouse air pump and the cylinder mounted on the front of the water tank. The cylinder contained a piston that was worked up and down by compressed air controlled by the driver from the front of the train when pushing. The piston rod can just be seen behind the top air pipe, also the link connected to a bar that ran down the length of the water tank with another link inside the cab that was connected to the regulator. At least that was how it was supposed to work, but in practice it didn't. So the 'pin' would be taken out and the fireman would control the engine by bell code from the driver. The conduit for the bell wiring can be seen down the side of the framing.

when the engine was rough with a dirty fire or tubes, or just a poor steamer, that things were a little different. This was when every trick of the trade would be tried, when you had to weigh up the odds of shutting that injector off to sacrifice the level in the boiler, concentrating all available heat on what you had and hoping against hope

20

that she would make steam to get the injector on again so as to recover what was lost, or at least keep what water was left. Sometimes after such a run, sacrificing water a drop at a time, you would reach the stage when there was a risk of damaging the firebox. Then the injector had to be turned on and left on. You then had to keep an eye on the steam and vacuum gauges, for if the steam pressure fell too low, the vacuum ejector would not have enough pressure to maintain the twenty-one inches required. The first sign of trouble would be a clicking from the ejector – an air clack jumping because the steam pressure would not be high enough to keep it off its seat. You got a look that could kill from the driver as he exerted just enough energy to open the large ejector valve and keep the brake off.

In 1949 I was called up for National Service, two years away from the footplate. But having the choice, I opted for the next best: the Royal Navy as a stoker. I felt that the two years away could be put to good use and further my knowledge of

boilers and steam engines. I had visions of stokers stripped to the waist, feeding tons of coal into ever-consuming boilers, with that frightening character, the Chief Stoker, pacing the 'plates', urging his black sweating crew to 'feed those boilers'. I was in for a surprise. Instead, I learned about oil-burning boilers, type Admiralty Three Drum, condensers, evaporators and steam turbines – not much good for my railway career.

11. Bournemouth yard shunter, G6 no. 30260, outside Bournemouth shed in March 1956. The MT chalked on the side of the bunker was put there by the boiler washers after washing out the boiler. She would have to be filled by hose through the injector overflow before lighting up. The overflow for the fireman's injector can be seen between the driving and trailing wheels; note how it is bent inwards to safeguard the shunters from steam and water. With this particular engine we were lucky enough to have a vacuum brake. A similar engine stationed at Dorchester was still braked with the hand brake, the fireman having to wind the brake handle furiously on and off at the shunter's command. The brake handle is just visible by the head lamp inside the cab. Notice how high from the footplate it is – a short fireman would be winding at practically shoulder height.

Keeping steam on a naval warship was much easier than on a railway steam engine. At the call for 'More steam' it was only a matter of 'flashing' up another burner, snapping open the air supply to the burner and briskly shouting out 'Up number four, sir', or whatever the number happened to be. Boiler water was controlled by a valve similar to the domestic water cistern, a pump providing the head of water. A close watch had to be kept on the water gauge for any failures, though. Unlike the steam engine, all the steam that had passed through the turbines was condensed back to water and returned to the water tanks, and evaporators would be used to top up with treated salt water. Every hour fuel and water tanks would be dipped and their contents logged. The plates on the boiler room decks were constantly being wiped over; cleanliness in a ship's boiler room took second place only to the conserving of water. What a difference to a steam engine.

1951 saw my return to the footplate, not a lot wiser than when I had left, but eager to resume my chosen career. Mr Bulleid's Channel Packets were now on the main line at Bournemouth. These new locomotives steamed so freely that the top link firemen would boast about going to London and back without cleaning the fire at Nine Elms, forgetting that the loco had probably also been to Weymouth and back before they took it over at Bournemouth. Anyway, by the time we came to dispose of them they had probably consumed about eight or nine tons of coal and been in full steam for almost sixteen hours. It was nothing to have clinker right up to the ring of the firebox door, and forty-nine square feet of this took some shifting. As these engines had not yet been fitted with drop grates, again everything had to be thrown out by shovel. Here again, by the time you had done this, the fire would be nearly out, and you could be chasing around for old sleepers to get it going

again. As I was still in the senior goods link my running experience with these engines was limited, but enough to convince me of their power.

In the summer of 1952 I was promoted to the 'push and pull' link, affectionately known as the 'lug and shove' or 'brush up and take water' gang. This link was something of a turning point: before, we had been performing the more menial tasks at the depot, but this was the first link consisting entirely of running work with passengers. Just a Drummond tank with two or sometimes three push and pull coaches and the longest run being from Bournemouth West to Brockenhurst – close on 32 miles – doesn't sound much but with the 'tools' we had it could be harder than going to London and back with a big 'un. I've always reckoned that this was the worst link at Bournemouth. Like the top link, however, we had our own regular engines, mine being 30057.

We also had two trips over the Swanage line out of Bournemouth West and the Central, and one trip over the Lymington branch where there was a depot at the end similar to Swanage but under the jurisdiction of Eastleigh.

So for two years this was my job; earliest turn at 04.25, the latest one finishing at 00.30, as far as Brockenhurst one way and Swanage the other. The fact that for half of the day I was on my own with the driver out of the way up front, giving me sole control of the engine, made the job bearable. All this after six years in the grade of fireman. Such was the strict enforcement of 'senior men – senior work' at Bournemouth. I shall always remember the Christmas of 1953, when on the 24th I was booked a one-way trip to Waterloo, returning home on the cushions (i.e. as a passenger). The driver was a top link man and refused to take me because I was a tank gang fireman! What a difference from later attitudes.

12. No. 35030, 'Elder Dempster Lines', the last of the Merchant Navy stable, in August 1957. What a change from the Drummonds and Maunsells that we had been brought up on! The sheer size of these engines was quite frightening, but once under way, with that massive, 49 square feet of firebox to be fed, all sense of size was forgotten. The top link had these engines from new, and never ceased to talk about the free running and steaming. A bad point in the design was the valleys each side of the coal hold. These were meant to contain the fire irons, but were always getting filled with coal. Also, the sand boxes either side of the nameplate were difficult to fill and much sand would drop on to the driving crankpin below. Since the 'Bournemouth Belle' was one of our prestige trains, I would have thought that clean route-indicating discs would be fitted. and where is the 'Bournemouth Belle' headboard?

2
Main Line Fireman

In the summer of 1954 I moved up to the number three link, the bottom rung of main line work. This was the beginning of the most interesting and thrilling period of my firing career. At last I was going to feel the roll of a Nelson at speed, not just for short bursts but for long distances; at last I would climb on to the footplate of a Pacific as the fireman, not as an onlooker or coaling boy.

My driver, Freddie, was an entirely different kettle of fish from my previous mate. He enjoyed a good joke and was indeed one of the jolliest drivers at Bournemouth; he was also one of the most efficient. If he did a job, it was done to perfection, and he expected no less of me. Even so, he never questioned my work or checked that I had done so and so, and this made for a happy team. It really was a pleasure going to work.

I had not previously worked beyond Eastleigh, but in this link we had a couple of London trips on Sundays, worked the 'Royal Wessex' between Bournemouth and Weymouth, and worked over the Salisbury and Templecombe roads, not to mention any extra London jobs such as excursions. There was also the opportunity to cover any temporary vacancies in the two top links. This meant that I spent quite a few weeks away from my regular driver.

The top link drivers that I had looked at in awe

when a young hand had by now long since retired; the top drivers were now those that were in the push and pull gang when I started. (Even so, many drivers retired without even reaching the top link.) I didn't regard the top men as frightening as those of the old school – this may seem strange to anybody with no knowledge of the footplate, but ask any driver what the old boys were like and you'll invariably be told what tartars they were. This brings to mind some of the old Nine Elms drivers that used to frequent Bournemouth in those days. They knew more about their engines than many fitters; if a repair had to be carried out on the engine before the return trip, they'd make sure it was done properly.

A story I heard many years ago concerning one of these London drivers typifies the sort of men they were. This happened before the war when the driver was the top man and his word was never questioned.

This particular driver was working a train to Bournemouth during the early evening of Christmas Eve and going up Pokesdown bank the engine developed a roar up the chimney. He managed to struggle into Bournemouth and the loco was taken on shed for examination. I doubt if he needed to be told what was wrong; she had blown a hole in one of the pistons, the result of water being drawn into the steam chest. He had

13. No. 34039, 'Boscastle', at Eastleigh works, undergoing a complete refit in May 1955. So often they would be turned out of the works just soled and heeled, as we would say, but this time she is having the lot. Note the superheater tubes lying in front. Steam from the regulator valve on top of the boiler was admitted to the saturated side of the header in the smokebox, and through these tubes that were inserted into the large smoke tubes. As reheated and dried out steam it would enter the superheated side of the header and thence to the steam chest. This accounts for the time it took a superheated engine to decide to move after the regulator was opened.

missed his last train back to Waterloo and the next one was the Mail. Well, this driver didn't fancy getting home at about 5 am on Christmas morning so he had the fitters remove the eccentric crank and the union link, knock out the gudgeon pin and remove the connecting rod. The combination lever and eccentric rod were tied securely to prevent them swinging about and the piston was pushed right forward with a piece of sleeper wedged behind the crosshead. The damaged cylinder now became an extension of the main steam chest and so, with all the bits and pieces slung in the back of the tender, off he went, light engine to London, taking a pinch bar in case he was stopped and the old girl wouldn't take steam on the good side. That was how determined the driver was to get home for his Christmas Eve drink.

As I've mentioned, my driver was very efficient. His watch was always one minute fast and this meant we had a minute to recover each time we left a station. He used much more water and coal than he need have done, but at least he ensured he

14. Probably the most serious collision ever to happen at Bournemouth. Charlie Johnson was the driver of H15 no. 30485 and was thrown out of his cab. He was unhurt but complained bitterly about his smashed watch. His fireman was thrown against the boiler front, smashing his head against the lubricator. The other engine involved, King Arthur no. 30783, has been drawn back almost clear of the picture. She had her right cylinder ripped off the framings but miraculously remained on the line. Mr Collins, the depot master at Bournemouth, is shown in the picture with his foot on the rail. In front of him, in uniform, is Mr Vic Rook, the traffic inspector, who would remain in evidence until the job was finished, no matter how long it took. Mr Rook was one of the last of a now extinct breed, a dedicated railwayman who commanded and got respect from all who had dealings with him.

14. C. P. Boocock

was always on time at stops. I really had to bend my back and give of my best, but still, this was my job – not to question, but to provide the steam when and how it was needed. He knew the name of every signal, block post, station and crossing throughout our area – no mean feat. If we were waiting for time, he would hand me his book containing all the 'gen' and recite it to me. Sometimes, as happens in all messrooms, he would ask someone, 'What's the name of the intermediate signal past so and so?' and was highly delighted if the person in question didn't know. One driver, when asked a question on a certain track layout, replied, 'Look mate, when it unfolds before me, so I recognise it.' This was to me a gem of an answer, one that I was to appreciate even more later on.

To emphasise this point, I recall the evening of August Bank Holiday Monday, 1954. I was working the 20.30 ex Waterloo with another driver who also considered himself well up on route knowledge. As this was an extra train, we were delayed and the first clear signals were not until Hampton Court Junction. As the result of these delays in the suburbs the fire was down on the bars, and with a tender full of Nine Elms

15. No. 34004 on the turntable at Bournemouth. For a main line depot this table left much to be desired. It was built on the site of an old pond, and the old drivers always reckoned that this was why Bournemouth table was so bad, the bed being able to flex and distort according to the weather conditions. When I first started the table was turned by hand, but at the end of 1950 a vacuum-operated mechanism was fitted – note the 'Hogger' pipe on the right of the picture to connect to the engine.

16. No. 76065 running into Templecombe Junction, with the tank engine waiting to drop on to the train to pilot it back up the bank into Templecombe station. Before setting back up to the station the fireman on 76065 would have to put a tail lamp on the front of the engine, or at night turn a headlamp to red. Once the pilot was attached, its driver would blow a 'crow' on the whistle to be answered by the train engine; this would be the signal to proceed with the movement, signals permitting. On the return to Bournemouth the procedure was reversed.

special dust I hadn't been able to prepare it properly. This called for dart and pricker action to lift the fire in an endeavour to get it hot before it disappeared up the chimney. So it was a case of fanning the special dust into the firebox and opening and shutting the fire door by hand, between shovelfuls. Through Horsham we were down to less than half a glass of water, so I eased the injector on, cutting it down as fine as possible and prepared myself to accept the fact that this was going to be one of those trips; I was really going to earn my mileage that night. The engine was 35008 before rebuilding and I remember that the generator wasn't working and the paraffin gauge lamp was tied to the Klingerflow gauge glass with worsted trimming. If that wasn't enough, the hydraulic lever wouldn't stop at the cut-off the driver set and so he was working the lever all the time. With all this going on, things weren't looking too bright.

Suddenly, the old girl gave a kick to the right and all hell was let loose. She thumped, banged, rolled and did everything but lie down. Coupled with this, we were lit up with electric flashes all around the cab. I stood in the middle of the footplate, hanging on to the manifold valves. Eventually we shuddered to a stand just short of a signal and through the twilight I could see the station ahead.

'What station's that up ahead?' I asked.

'I don't know, mate,' the driver replied. 'I'll go to the box after I've examined the engine and find out where we are.'

This particular driver could list every signal, parrot fashion, but distract him from his job, put him down somewhere at night and he was lost. I learned something from this.

In case you're worried about 35008, she'd thrown her trailing coupling rod from the driving crankpin, left hand side. The journal on the driving crankpin had split right down the centre and the whole trailing coupling rod, flaying around loose, had smashed the ashpan to pieces on that side. All the casing and pipes in the vicinity were also smashed, with the remaining rods bent on both sides. I dread to think what the inside motion and chain-driven valve gear looked like but amidst all this, somehow the leading coupling rod remained in place, hanging on to the crankpin with half a journal.

The engine was immobile and when the fitters eventually arrived on the scene they had to cut off all the rods. As it was one of the busiest nights of the year we had to wait until every train had passed us on the down local until we were pulled back to the station in the rear. A Lord Nelson that was being worked by Eastleigh men back to the depot and had been delayed was put on the front, and we took it through to Bournemouth. As the Eastleigh men had had no reason to know that their engine would be called upon to work a train when they left Nine Elms, they had not taken much coal. Running light with a Nelson didn't warrant much coal but fortunately the coal that we had was good Eastleigh Welsh coal and so we didn't do too badly. Arriving at Bournemouth at 03.30, we found there was no relief so we had to work the empty train through to Broadstone to berth it. When we eventually arrived back at Bournemouth depot we were worn out and hungry. As for disposal duties, I couldn't have done it for a hundred pounds.

The duties involved over the Templecombe road we worked with small Standards, one of the 76s and not, thank goodness, one of the Midland engines. The route was out of the West over our own territory to Broadstone and then branching northwards on to the Somerset and Dorset road, climbing up through the hills between the eighth and ninth holes of Broadstone Golf Course.

This was a railway that I'd seen so many times but had never worked over, even though it was such a short distance from Bournemouth, but what a joy it was to travel over this pretty piece of line to Templecombe. If anywhere was steeped in Victoriana this was. At one station the local bobby lit the single paraffin lamp in the morning and blew it out after the last train at night. At another station the signalman was invariably in the middle of cleaning out his pigs

or fowls when we whistled at the distant. Vegetables and fruit could be ordered for the end of the week and eggs or cider could be picked up on the return journey to Bournemouth. Traditions, equipment and railway life had not changed over this line since the day it was built. Summer evenings saw the locals hanging around the stations to watch the comings and goings of the trains even though the railway was no longer their only connection with the outside world. I had the impression that as soon as our tail lamp disappeared from sight, everyone went home to bed.

Another noticeable thing about the old S & D was the fact that the railway was built round the hills and not through them; I suppose in those far-off days it was cheaper to buy the land than to dig tunnels. One station, Spetisbury, was balanced on the side of a hill overlooking the village.

Most of this road was single line, the token being picked up and exchanged by machine. This machine consisted of a pair of jaws, not unlike a crocodile's, with three 'teeth' that could fold back and spring up again. The wicked-looking contraption was hung out of the side of the engine but on the Midland engines it was part of the loco with various fittings to swing or slide it in and out. However, on our Standards a bracket was welded to the tender and the catcher had to be dropped into position prior to exchanging the tablet or token. Some West Country's that worked over this road, had a bracket fixed to the top step on the driver's side, conveniently placed so as to take the skin off anyone's ankles.

A pilot engine would always be attached when we arrived at Templecombe junction to pull us back up into the old LSWR station. We were relieved by Bath men and we in turn would take over the pilot engine. Meanwhile the Waterloo to Exeter train would pull in, with the engine hardly to a stand before the fireman was up in the tender shovelling over his coal for the next part of the journey. As the engine had worked out of Nine Elms, it didn't take much imagination to know what sort of coal he had left to perform with. As they pulled out on the up gradient, sanders working full bore, the fireman would still be up there in the tender until they were out of sight.

If anyone earned their money in those days, these firemen certainly did. We thought that ours was a hard main line but our conditions were much more favourable than those of the West of England firemen. They took over at Salisbury with a far from clean fire, all the good coal used and the worst part of the journey in

17. T9 no. 30300, a class which we knew as 'Greyhounds', running into Daggons Road. The 1900/01-built series of engines had wider splashers to accommodate the connecting rods. Note the six-wheel tender as opposed to the 'water-cart' version some of the T9s were fitted with. This platform at Daggons Road was used for both the up and down trains. Try finding that solitary paraffin lamp on a winter's night when it is raining and blowing a gale – it was not too bad running in this direction towards Salisbury, but running in the other way the driver was blind to the platform.

18. The Schools class, one of the most successful engines built, were not powerful getting away with a train because the driving wheels tended to slip. But get them going and pull the valves up into a short cut-off and they would fly. They were designed for express work with loads of 300 tons or ten bogies, and as such nothing would catch them. But the war years thwarted the designer's intentions, and fourteen and fifteen bogies were the regular load between Bournemouth and Waterloo. I have even seen a train of seventeen bogies leave Bournemouth headed by a Schools. Here, no. 30902, 'Wellington', is speeding past Basingstoke with an up train. Note the distance between the wheels under the engine, with the trailing driving wheel placed right back under the cab, and what must have been the longest coupling rod on any engine. To my way of thinking all the weight is on the driving wheel with not enough on the trailing wheel. No wonder they 'danced'.

31

front of them.

Back on the Templecombe pilot, we would wait for the Bath–Bournemouth train and once again change over with the crew. Then, a run back home with another 76, through the farm lands, round the hills, over and under old stone bridges: Henstridge, Stalbridge, Sturminster, Newton, Shillingstone, Blandford, Spetisbury and Bailey Gate. Finally, through Corfe Mullen junction and back on to the Southern at Broadstone.

So to the summer of 1955 and the rail strike. One good thing about it was the weather. Apart from that it was a sheer waste of time and money; the drivers got a few shillings increase out of it, and I do mean a few shillings. We firemen got nothing. We returned to work in the middle of the third week, back to rusty engines with the handrails and fire irons red with rust. Some fires had been left to burn out, so the ashes and half-burnt coal had to be thrown out of the boxes before the engines could be prepared for service.

19. Les Elsey

19. No. 34094, 'Mortehoe', with the down 'Royal Wessex' getting away from Winchester in June 1951. At this time one of Bournemouth's prestige trains, it was still worked by Bournemouth top link with their own regular engines. A few years after this, Bournemouth top link ceased to have their own engines and a regular engine was worked on this turn, always the best steed at the depot. As an engine came fresh off shops she would be booked on this turn until the next off-shops arrival. Note the swivelling lids over the sandboxes. This was supposed to be an improvement on the original sliding covers that would not slide.

20. Lord Nelson no. 30864, 'Sir Martin Frobisher', with the 10.40 am up from Bournemouth, waiting to get away from Southampton for the last sprint to Waterloo. As a fireman this was my favourite class of engine: master these and you could make anything steam. To me the Lord Nelsons were the complete steam locomotive. Note the long slender connecting rod and eccentric rod as compared to a Pacific. They would burn far less coal than a Pacific, and it was possible, due to the design of the footplate and shovelling tray, to work all the way to Waterloo and not drop a piece of coal on the footplate. At speed the footplate set so high and far behind the rear wheel would roll at amazing angles, a sensation that would make the blood pound with excitement.

By the end of that week we were back to normal and the topic in the drivers' cabin was what we would get out of the industrial action. Should we have returned or stopped out? Whatever the arguments, they were soon forgotten and the main conversation reverted to our mutual interest, the steam engine.

We had been nationalised now for seven years and, apart from the renumbering of the engines and the enginemen's badges which were no longer issued to new firemen, very little change had taken place on the Southern.

Mr Bulleid's engines were deteriorating, both internally and externally. Many had burn patches on the castings where they had caught alight due to the oil-soaked dirt that seemed to be everywhere. The valve gear oil baths leaked at every joint, evident at stations where engines came to a stand. Hydraulic reversers no longer maintained the cut-off where it was required, some creeping back into reverse while the engine was travelling forward at speed. Some suddenly dropped forward into full gear, and the sudden increase in the volume of steam being allowed through the wide open valves would drag boiler water into the cylinders. By the time the cylinder cocks had been opened and the regulator valve closed, half a boiler of water would be gone.

Even the cylinder cocks gave up the ghost on some engines. As they were operated by a system of rods and levers, slight wear in the joints resulted in difficulty opening the cocks or even in their refusing to close. You could often see the fireman at stations armed with a coal pick, hammering at the various levers and rods around the cylinders while the driver pushed on the cocks' handle in an effort to close them before the 'right away' was given.

Our King Arthurs and Nelsons did not seem to get any worse, often working in place of Pacifics on hard duties. It even reached a stage when some top firemen preferred a Nelson on the main line: they knew that although more skill was needed they wouldn't shift half as much coal.

21. No. 75072 running into Sturminster Newton on the S. and D. road, the whole scene so typical of the old 'Slow and Dirty'. No hurry – take your time. The signalman is strolling up to the end of the platform to exchange tablets with the driver. He could have changed the tablet (visible in its pouch in his right hand) at his signal box, but how much nicer to stroll up to the engine and exchange a few words with the driver, to get first-hand knowledge of the outside world. Note the Cotswold stone of the water tower, also the brickwork around the top to raise the tank with the introduction of bigger engines.

21. Hugh Ballantyne

3
Number Two Link

During the summer of 1956 I took leave of number three link and progressed up to number two which in my opinion was the best at Bournemouth. It was particularly favoured by the second link firemen because all the top link men were passed for driving duties. So when a top fireman was taken off his London trip to perform a driving duty, the nearest fireman in number two to the signing-on time filled the vacancy. As well as being the first to grab the crumbs that fell from the top link table, number two had rostered London work with an Oxford thrown in for good measure. Also, as the top link had no rostered Sunday work, all the London trips were in number two link on the Sabbath. All in all, financially, number two was equal to, if not better than, number one.

Why was trip-work so eagerly sought? Well, we were paid for miles worked with an extra hour for every fifteen miles over 140. This meant that a London trip was worth an extra five and a half hours' pay with Oxford an extra four and a half: a very fair arrangement if you were in the top two links but most unfair for men in the lower ones, who after all were surely entitled to earn a reasonable living. There were firemen up to six years older than me in number three link, but these men were restricted to earn less than I

could, solely because I had applied for a job a few months before they did. This could also be said of the drivers. Men of forty years had to live as did men of sixty, although the younger man probably had more commitments such as a family to support. And wasn't a driver in his forties just as capable of taking a train to London and back, and physically wasn't he more suited? This argument was frequently discussed in the drivers' cabin and sides were taken according to where you were on the roster, i.e. those chosen few who were permitted to perform on the main line, against those who weren't.

Take, for instance, a junior driver who had just completed his firing days. He would have finished in the top link knowing the road like the back of his hand, yet as a junior driver in the bottom link it would be years and years before he went up to London again. But put him straight back on the main line as a driver with a senior fireman and what an ideal team. They would be almost the same age, both equal in health, eyesight and everything else. However, the law of the depot meant that the senior man on both sides of the footplate had the cream and I was now one of the elite twenty-four, so I did not complain – this was what I'd waited twelve years for.

No man was allowed to work more than three

trips per week, excluding Sundays, so if Dame Fortune smiled on you it was possible to get a trip on the Sunday plus three in the week. This would add up to fourteen hours for the Sunday and four trips at five and a half hours making a total of thirty-six hours' extra pay on top of the week's wages. The pay for a top fireman was then £9 12s and for a top driver £11 11s, both after six years in the grade, so it was easy to see why trip-work was so popular. However, the one bad point about trip-work was that you were not paid for any overtime unless it exceeded the mileage; then you were paid the overtime but lost the mileage. So if you were late back with a trip owing to fog or some other disruption to the service, you worked the extra hours for nothing.

Number two link was also blessed with the cover turns at 8 am and 1 pm. These were to cover the non-arrival of drivers or firemen for a London or Oxford turn. The running foreman was not permitted to use these cover men for any duty during the first four hours in case they were called out. There were four hours in which to drink tea, play cards or catch up on the news of the depot; to watch the foreman cleaner chasing the cleaners just as he used to chase us eleven years ago. Was it that long ago? It didn't seem like it. Look – there's a new cleaner, just started (you can always spot them as they're the dirtiest,

not having learned the dodges yet). And look at that poor, weak-looking soul. Can't imagine him making a fireman.

'Does your Mum know you're here, son?'

Think yourself lucky that a top fireman even notices you're here. Don't you know that I'm the cover fireman, experienced enough to go anywhere, to work on any engine?

But wait . . . This was the very attitude that I despised, the attitude of those old drivers, most of them now retired but one or two still living on past glories.

'Don't worry, son. Your wrists will get thick and your shoulders broad. You'll swing a shovel and handle a Nelson's long fire-shovel as good as anyone. You'll get sworn at by the drivers and you'll sweat and find out what an ungodly hour 3 am is in the middle of winter. You'll climb on the bottom rung of that long ladder I'm now nearing the top of, a top that I can see but is still out of reach.'

This may seem dramatic, but it is how it was, how it felt when you reached number two link.

As I've mentioned before, in this link we 'filled in' for the top firemen, so I fired to practically all the top twelve drivers. One fireman who didn't get on very well with his driver was always willing to change turns with me if I had a day shift compared with his early or late turn. But drivers were as different as chalk and cheese. Some would very nearly lift the chimney off while others would do the same amount of work, still run to time and burn less coal.

One heavy-handed driver was nicknamed 'Stair-rod' because he always had red stair-rods sticking out of his chimney – the speed with which hot ashes left the chimney made them look just like stair-rods, and not just one or two but hundreds.

Another driver, who was one of the few remaining who still lived on past glories, is

22. King Arthur no. 30765, 'Sir Gareth', rounding Northam curve with the Newcastle in August 1957. This was the first of the Bournemouth duties to return from Oxford, the same engine being worked up and back. No. 30765 was a regular engine for this duty, and kept pretty well up together. The tender would be very low on coal now, and providing the driver stopped right for water at Southampton, with the water bag hanging straight into the tender, the fireman would scramble over the last of his coal for what could be the hardest part of the journey, Southampton to Bournemouth. More than once I have known the Newcastle engine to come off on arrival at Bournemouth with not enough coal left to work to Bournemouth West.

worth a mention if only because of the fact that he was a character in his own way. He would arrive on duty with the remains of a hand-rolled cigarette clamped between his lips. Any greeting would be answered with a grunt and anyone who was in his way would be shouldered aside. How dare anyone obstruct the passage of one of the top drivers on the Southern Region! One serge jacket pocket contained a bottle of cold tea, the other bulged with his sandwiches. At the appointed time he would proceed to the up platform, weaving his way through the waiting passengers, his fireman tagging along behind. He would work up to London and back with the minimum of words passing his lips. Back at Bournemouth he would step off the engine with not a word for his relief and the same cigarette end, by now as black as the coal that he'd blasted through the chimney with such wild abandon, still clasped between his lips. This same cigarette had been rolled back and forth along his lips all day long, only to be removed to take a swig of the tea bottle or to take a bite of his cheese sandwiches.

The first time I worked with this driver, I remember waiting in the cabin as though it was my first firing turn. What would he say about not having his own mate? I picked up my bag and sidled up to him to let him know that I was ready to follow him to the station.

A thick Dorset accent (he was a native of Wareham) said, 'Theesun my mate?' He knew damned well I was – he could read the alteration sheet.

'Yes, mate.' I followed his steps to the end of the platform feeling like a sheep going to its doom. How would I perform today? Hope we had a good engine. Would he speak again to let me know how he felt about having a strange fireman?

We stepped on to the engine, with the crew we'd relieved watching his eyes wander over the footplate looking for something to complain about. I watched the steam gauge, hoping she wasn't going to lift her safety valves. The water was just below the top nut so she'd take a drop to keep her quiet if necessary. He looked over at me. Was he going to holler, 'Get that so-and-so injector on', 'Keep her quiet' or what? One thing at least, he recognised I was there. Then with a gesture towards the firebox he shouted, 'I'll make t'oles, theesun fill 'em up.'

On my life, those were the only words he spoke to me all day, but regardless of this we had a good trip up and back. It was a good engine and I knew that I was on trial, so I gave of my best. Back in Bournemouth cabin once again, I washed off and watched him finish off his ticket. As he stood up and turned towards the door, he looked at me with a slight smile on his face. He knew that his reputation had worried me but I believe I had proved myself as I was often

23. Rebuilt Merchant Navy no. 35018, 'British India Line', leaving Bournemouth West with the 'Belle'. Steam locomotives had different characters even though they were all built the same, and 35018 was one of the good ones in her class. Bournemouth West as in this picture is now completely removed from the face of the earth; there is no sign whatsoever of the station that once stood there, and a new motorway now passes over this site. At the time of this photograph Bournemouth top link turned and prepared the 'Belle' engine themselves, it being one of their days with no trip to London. They would get relieved by their own link at Bournemouth, so any complaints were kept in the link.

24. Unrebuilt Bulleid Pacific no. 35017, 'Belgian Marine', on the disposal pit at Nine Elms in 1950. The loco is in blue livery. Noticeable is the absence of clinkers – I have seen the clinker piled up so high on either side of the line that it was possible to step straight off the footplate on to the top of the piles of clinkers and ashes. The coming of the drop grate engines played havoc with the concrete sides of the pits, rendering them out of action for days on end while hasty repairs were made. Between the pit roads can be seen the foundations of the ramp for the old coal stage, prior to the hopper.

booked with him and he later became quite chatty once I'd been accepted.

Another driver would rush to work, arriving about half an hour before time, park his push-bike and make a beeline for his locker where he kept his cherished pipe and tobacco. A fill-up and then sign on for duty, relaxing in the driver's cabin and puffing away at his first smoke of the day. He wasn't allowed to smoke at home so he made up for it at work. I often wondered what he did on his rest days.

One driver, who wasn't tall enough to open a Lord Nelson's regulator fully, would come across to the fireman's side and leap up and grasp the end of the regulator and swing on it, feet clear of the footplate. This was all right until the Nelson slipped, then he would scamper back to his own side, leap up and grab that end and swing on it again to close it. He'd then go through the routine again, shouting at me something about 'These engines were made for

25. No. 35021, 'New Zealand Line', waiting to leave Oxford, with a through train for the Eastern Region passing through from the Southern behind no. 34097. Unlike the Southern, head codes on the GWR did not describe the route but the class of train. One each side of the buffer beam denotes a main line passenger. Note the odd shapes of the GWR signal arms: there never seemed to be two the same length, and they still retained the lower quadrant arms.

blankety-blank giants'. On a Pacific he would climb up the boiler front with both feet and heave on the regulator.

Starting away on the down road at Brock-enhurst was always a pantomime. More often than not Pacifics wouldn't start from here first time, so this meant reversing the engine, setting back a few feet, putting her into fore gear and trying again. Sometimes an engine would need two or three attempts before getting away. This driver would open the steam cocks and, being too impatient to wait for the steam chest to empty of steam, would strain and sweat to get

40

her into reverse gear; anybody who's tried to reverse a Pacific with the steam chest full will know how hard it is to turn the reverser. By the time he'd wound her back to mid-gear the steam-operated cocks would open, the piston valves would free the steam and the lever would then wind back easily. He would close the cocks and give her steam to set her back, then go through the same performance to get her into fore gear. I used to sit and watch all this and think, 'Why doesn't he have a little patience and wait a few seconds for the cocks to open to empty the steam chest? It would be so easy then.' Eventually getting away from Brockenhurst, he would thrash the engine unmercifully up Sway bank, getting his own back on the engine with never a thought for the large quantities of fire and water being discharged through the chimney.

Then there were the drivers who would snatch the shovel out of your hands when things weren't going too well. As a rule this happened between Micheldever and the top of the bank. You'd nursed the engine from Southampton through Eastleigh, Winchester, passing Wallers Ash and Weston, losing an inch of water here

26. The Urie-built S15 engines were good reliable machines, capable of passenger work or goods. This class we would have on the Nine Elms goods, with that tall chimney barking out the exhaust. Having 5 ft 7 in. driving wheels they really had to be pushed to time express trains. Note the dark strip down the tender directly behind the footplate gangway, which was also fitted to the Nelsons and Schools. It was a tender water gauge, having a series of holes drilled up the tender. A small handle on the tender opened up the water to these holes and gave a reading on the tender content. Unfortunately they were unreliable owing to the lack of use, and the holes would get filled up with dirt and rust. No. 30496 is leaving Southampton Central on a local train train composed of L & SWR stock in 1956.

and gaining a few pounds of steam there. And so you'd performed until the point of no return, as a rule around Popham, sacrificing water for steam until there would now be less than half a glass of water. With the regulator open it was inadvisable to shut the injector. If the driver closed the regulator the water would drop out of sight in the glass. By now the steam pressure had dropped forty or fifty pounds below maximum. If a Pacific she would still plod on, a Nelson in this condition would lose power and speed, and a King Arthur could still be coaxed to keep time. This was the sign for these drivers, all in their sixties, to snatch the shovel, attempt to shake off thirty years and try to do better than you had done for the last twenty miles of uphill climb. Talking with other firemen about such situations, I found that some of them took umbrage

27. Rebuilt Battle of Britain no. 34053, 'Sir Keith Park', passing Wogret Junction, the branch line to Swanage showing behind the signal box. This part of the branch is still in use to serve the oil terminal at Furzebrook, although the box is no longer there, the points being worked from a ground frame alongside the points. I do not like that front coupling hanging down – it should have been hung up after being used. It would not have taken a few seconds to secure and can only denote a lazy fireman. But any mishap with that coupling would fall heaviest on the shoulders of the driver, as he is in charge of the engine and responsible for the fireman.

28. No. 34087, '145 Squadron', one engine that always seemed to be a good 'un, steaming through Pokesdown with the 'Bournemouth Belle', passing the stopper on the up local. The fireman on the local has not trimmed his coal at all and it looks very dangerous – another duty of the fireman that, through laziness, would be overlooked. The driver on the 'Belle' has eased off steam after the climb out of Bournemouth for the run down and through Christchurch, giving his fireman the chance to get the boiler water back for the hard pound up Hinton Admiral bank.

28. Mike Esau

and would tell the driver that if he wanted to do the firing he could do it for the rest of the day. For myself, I would sit down and think, 'Well, if he wants to try his luck, let him get on with it.'

Then there was the driver who insisted that the fireman sit down between bouts of firing. He'd say, 'Take advantage of every opportunity to rest, my son, you have to spend enough time on your feet as it is.' If you'd had a good trip he would never fail to thank you at the end of the day, and always within earshot of others. He wanted others to know that he treated his fireman as a human being and not just as the character who was there to shovel coal. This driver was one of the best I ever fired to; he knew the engine backwards, likewise the rule book, and if anyone tried to pull a fast one over him or his mate with, say, a bad preparation, heaven help them.

Another driver always insisted on doing half the firing regardless of what train or turn it was. The first time I was booked with him on a London trip, I'd heard of his reputation but believed he only carried on in this manner with his regular mate. But no, as we pulled out of Bournemouth and I was taking stock of the fire and getting ready to perform, he came across the footplate and said in his well-spoken manner, 'I will do the firing going up and you will do it coming back.' I declined the offer as I had never driven an engine any further than up and down the yard, even after twelve years on the job.

A lot of firemen jumped in the driver's seat at every opportunity, and I know of some who would always do their driver's oiling in order to have a 'go' on the regulator. I always had enough to do with my own job without doing the driver's as well. Anyway, this driver informed me that this was his regular procedure and he didn't intend to change it because of me, and if I didn't have the confidence to do the job now I never would have – also he liked to keep his waist-line down. So each time I was booked with this driver, like other firemen I had to do half the driving. I remember I used to watch him sweating away with the shovel thinking to myself, 'Why doesn't he do this or why doesn't he do that?' My hands would itch to get hold of the shovel. He used to brush all the coal dust on the footplate up against the boiler front, then wash it down between the boiler and footplate with the 'pep' pipe. The draught would then blow it back up in the form of black mud, covering us both.

Then we had the driver who would make weird signs without saying a word. Waving his right forefinger in the air in a circular motion meant, 'Would you please turn the injector off, old chappie, I consider there is enough water in the boiler?' or 'Put the blasted thing on' if he thought it was about time it went on. A thumb and finger held up in the air a few inches apart meant 'Open the door a little wider'. This would be because he considered the engine was emitting too much smoke after a fire-up. Another sign, he would stand up and brush his overalls down with flicks of a cloth, conveying to the observant fireman that there was dust blowing around and it was about time the footplate was dampened down.

Finally, let's not forget the driver who could never read the scale on the reverser of the unconverted Pacifics. The numbers were punched on the top of a brass strip and constant rubbing through the years had made them difficult to

29. No. 34053, 'Sir Keith Park', on a winter's afternoon leaving Waterloo with the 1.30 pm departure. Les Gallon of Bournemouth, then a fireman, is no doubt contemplating the 108 miles that lie ahead before he can go home. Looking at the escape of steam around the steam chests, '53 does not look too bright. All that steam could be put to better use as she digs her heels in. Never mind, Les – all being well you shouldn't shift much more than two tons of coal, and over 4,000 gallons of water, in the next two hours. Then they'll let you go home.

read, so he would hand me a piece of chalk and ask me to mark off thirty-five and forty-five degrees. If an engine was worked between these points of cut-off I was in for a rough time, so I used to chalk marks on twenty-five and thirty-five. We would still time the train, consume much less coal and water, and I saved the BR pounds on their coal bill.

My driver was Joe Langdon, an ex-Plymouth and Nine Elms man. Being a 'Devon', he had started cleaning at Plymouth, gaining promotion to fireman at Nine Elms and then driver at Bournemouth. He had, incidentally, fired to my grandfather while at the Elms, and perhaps it was this triangle that made me hold Joe in such high esteem. Even now when I reminisce it is always my time with Joe that springs to the fore. He was master of the steam engine in every way. He knew the road better than any driver I'd fired to before, driving the engine according to the gradients. Working down from London with other drivers the regulator and valve cut-off would be set leaving Clapham curve and that's where it stopped, signals permitting, until shutting off for Worting Junction. But with Joe the regulator would be eased at Earlsfield, increased again at Raynes Park, eased down again at Berrylands and increased at West Byfleet for the climb through Woking to Pirbright, eased down again at Sturt Lane junction, increased after Farnborough. This way the engine would be worked with the minimum amount of effort, steam and water, and of course it made it easy for me. With a driver like Joe the main line was dead easy.

He had his own stopping mark for all the water columns, marks that I was to remember later on. The times at Southampton that I've had to hang on to the water bag, guiding it into the tender hole with my leg, only for it to catch on one of the cross members inside the tender and drench me. But not with Joe; he would stop right every time.

One of our London turns was up with the 08.46 from Bournemouth, and return with the 15.20 ex Waterloo. On the up trip we would run on the slow road from Basingstoke to Woking and just before Hook the 09.30 from Bournemouth would pass us on the fast road, being a non-stop from Southampton. It would give Joe great joy to open the engine up and catch the fast train. As a rule the engine on our turn was a West Country in poor condition. On the fast train would be a Channel Packet, all cleaned up because she worked the Belle on the return journey. The thrill of seeing two steam engines racing smokebox to smokebox has to be seen to be believed, good-humoured remarks being shouted between cabs.

The other London trip in our gang was up with the 14.40 two-hour train to Waterloo and back with the 19.30 ex Waterloo. An interesting point about this two-hour train was that when I first worked it with Joe it was allowed two hours and ten minutes from Bournemouth to Waterloo, then the new timetable came out re-timing these fast trains to two hours. I remember wondering how they could knock off ten minutes just like that, with the only concession being that the load was restricted to 300 tons. So when our turn came round to work the newly timed train I

30. The driver, having taken water at Southampton Central, secures the safety chain. It has been known for these water cranes to swing out over the main line in a high wind. The driver would now scramble back on to the footplate to be ready for the whistles from the station staff denoting that the train was ready to leave. It was always looked upon as bad practice to be still taking water when the station staff were ready for the off. If the engine was going to work through to Weymouth, she would have to be filled very nearly to the top, but if only as far as Bournemouth then water in the tap (i.e. about half a tender of water) would probably be enough, depending on the type of train.

was a bit apprehensive about what to expect. We arrived at Waterloo at 16.40 dead on two hours, I didn't work any harder and neither did the engine. I believe that had the train been reduced to one hour fifty-five minutes Joe would still have timed it just as easily, and this was without a speedometer, just his watch and his knowledge of the road.

The up York was one of the turns in number two link. We departed from Central at 11.26, the train being worked round from West by the lower link. Arrival at Oxford was 14.30, depar-ture from Oxford 15.35, arriving back at Bournemouth Central and relief at 18.36. As can be seen, we only had sixty-five minutes at Oxford. This was to uncouple from the train, get on to Oxford loco pit, clean the fire, take water, get the coal over from the back of the tender, make the fire up, turn the engine and get back to the station and couple on to the train for the return journey. All this in sixty-five minutes.

There was no allowance made for 'grub' time and many's the time that I've taken my sandwiches home again uneaten. Not having had enough time in the loco to build up a good fire, it

31. S. C. Nash

was into it from the start, unlike leaving Waterloo where we always had plenty of time in the Elms to get a good bottom to the fire, and not have to use valuable time shovelling over the coal. Also we nearly always had a young fireman at Nine Elms to assist us in turning the engine. But at Oxford loco we didn't have any help, regardless of how little time we had. Many times through delays on the up trip we've arrived at Oxford behind time, with the down service waiting on the other platform. It was then a case of a quick turn around and doing only the necessary jobs to the engine. This then meant a rough trip on the return, a dirty fire and every bit of coal having to be pulled while on the move before it could be shovelled into the firebox. Once again no time for physical needs, the only consolation being that Joe would have a chance to make the tea while I was coupling on.

This had been the routine on this turn for years, it being an accepted fact that if there was no time for a break before working back it was just too bad. Conditions of footplate service stated that no claim for a break could be made on mileage duties! This was the only turn at Bournemouth where this was applied. However this was 1957, not 1907, so we kicked up through every available source about the unfairness of

31. No. 30736, 'Excalibur', was the first of the Urie-built series of King Arthurs. Here she is passing Bramley with the 9.30 am Birkenhead–Bournemouth on 27 August 1955. As a rule these were good engines, but 30736 left much to be desired. She was quite easy to make steam, but was very weak and the drivers would have to burn much more coal to time the train. Despite this she was a regular engine on this duty for years. Note the different line of the cab roof, and the wide chimney. I have heard old drivers tell of the days when these were the main line engines at Bournemouth, and the then shedmaster set up the valves on them himself. They reckoned they were the best engines on the system then, and to leave one at a foreign depot was fatal – it would be weeks before she was returned to Bournemouth. The shedmaster, Mr Elliot, would heap blood and thunder on whoever kept one of his engines.

this turn and at long last something was done to improve it. Did I say improve? That is a matter of opinion, but at least we had an hour to ourselves and if we were late, time could be found for a quick bite.

The solution worked out by the powers that work out such things was that we would be relieved by a Great Western crew on arrival at Oxford, and would have a Great Western engine of the Hall or Grange class brought off shed on to the train. We would then work the return journey with it. The Southern engine was worked back later in the day to Basingstoke and then to Bournemouth with, I believe, a parcels train.

Joe and I were the first to work this new arrangement. I must admit we were both looking forward to the experience as neither of us had worked one of these engines before.

I remember the engine we had up that day. At this time there were two engines regularly booked on this turn, one being 30865, the Nelson with the valves coupled in pairs giving four beats to the wheel, the other 30736, a King Arthur that was as weak as a kitten. Each of these engines consumed more coal than others of its class, the Nelson because of the heavier beat, and the Arthur because she had to be worked that little bit harder. On the day in question we had the Arthur, and we worked to Oxford where we were relieved by the Oxford men.

We'd always commented on the cleanliness of the GWR engines, the brass on the chimney and regulator dome always shiny. It was going to be a treat to have a clean engine. Eventually our train arrived and I went out to watch the changing of engines. (Funny how we never tired of watching steam engines.) A magnificent Hall was de-trained and taken away to shed, and the most scruffy Grange we'd ever seen was setting back on to our train. So this was it – Joe and I climbed aboard taking stock of what we had to contend with. Joe asked where the hell they'd dug this old tub from, and we were informed that she'd been on pilot duties over the weekend.

I checked the water in the boiler and found she was full to the whistle; checking the fire I found it right up under the baffle plate so at least I had a good start; checked the injectors, no trouble there; the blower, that was O.K. How was the coal? Coal? What coal? We had a tenderful of those coconut-sized brickets, half cement, half coal dust. Well, I was going to have to make the

most of it. Great Western men worked trains with these engines and so could we.

We had the road, Joe had created the vacuum, the guard was whistling so off we went. We looked at each other as she blasted her way out of Oxford (a much quicker blast than the Arthur), waiting for her to lift her water as a Southern engine would with so much water in the boiler, but she didn't. Joe pulled the valves up and opened the regulator wide. Time I performed.

32. No. 34093, 'Saunton', taking water in Oxford loco in 1965. When I was on this turn with Driver Joe Langdon we would await our chance to slide quietly back under the coal stage and tip ourselves a couple of tubs of coal. The coalman would dash out from his hidey-hole, but by then it would be too late. It was not the fact that we Southern men were nicking their coal, but that he had two extra tubs to fill. However, this would give us a good start getting away from Oxford, and by the time I had shifted that ton of coal the fire would be hot enough to consume the small coal and dust that was left.

I used the dart and lifted the fire, forcing the dart down through to the bars. The fire had been made up for stand-by hours earlier, and the underneath had burned through. The brickets had caked together on the top, giving the impression of a box full of fire. So I had to shovel, and shovel I did – that darned great Western shovel would hold nearly half a hundredweight. The tender shovelling plate was level with the footplate, unlike the Southern engines where the plate was on a level with the fire door and it was just a case of a swing from A to B with the knees straight. On this engine every shovelful had to be lifted first, and believe me, after what I was used to it was hard work. Also with one of our engines I wouldn't need to get up into the tender to move the coal forward until Winchester or even Southampton, but with this old girl I was up there shovelling it forward at Reading and again at every stop. Also, as the tender carried less water than the Southern, we had to take on water at Basingstoke and Southampton, and by the time we'd reached Southampton the coal was back so far I needed a wheelbarrow to bring it forward!

Arriving at Bournemouth, three hours of hard graft behind us and blacker than we'd ever been, Joe and I agreed that we didn't go much on Western engines. One consolation though: no trip could be worse than the one we'd just had.

On the second trip to Oxford I made a point of asking the Great Western fireman what one had to do to make their engines steam. He said, 'Just keep loading the coal under the fire door, let the fire slope steeply to the front and let the blast do the rest. Keep the blower on hard all the time and the boiler water up to the whistle.'

Water to the whistle? This was feasible if the engine would take it. The more water in the boiler the less room left to fill with steam, so the only room left for steam was in the regulator dome. It was all so different from our engines where we had to keep the water no more than an inch from the top of the glass, two-thirds water, one-third steam. And what a blower; coupled with the fact that Western engines had twice the gap between the firebars compared with the Southerns, the blower would lift any fire off the bars, clinker and all. Considering the time these engines worked without having their fires cleaned, they needed it.

So I worked the fire as I'd been told, though this time I must admit that the engine handed over to us was far more typical of the Western engines, all brass and gleaming paintwork. This time we had a much better trip back to Bournemouth.

4
Promotion – And More Firing

This must take us up to the beginning of 1958. More and more men from other depots who were my seniority and age, particularly from Nine Elms, were now either passed firemen or registered drivers. I was still an ordinary fireman and this hurt my pride. Imagine being relieved at Waterloo by a pair of Nine Elms men and discovering that the driver used to shovel your coal over at the Elms! Here he was, driving regularly, and here was I still on the shovel, still doing the same job. Then again, to see men working trains from London to Bournemouth as drivers, who had started cleaning at the same time as I had, helped to bring home the fact that I had to start looking for promotion.

The third rail was coming through to Bournemouth from Sturt Lane and dieselisation was at the back of everybody's mind at this time. This subject had been discussed in the drivers' cabin hundreds of times since I'd been on the job. Electrification of the Bournemouth road was on the books before the Second World War. I can remember when I was cleaning that drivers talked about the end of steam on the Bournemouth road.

Reluctant as I was to leave my home town, I could see no other way of getting to the grade of driver. There were drivers reaching retiring age but there were still drivers queuing up to fill the vacancies created, waiting to move from other depots to Bournemouth to retire. These were keeping promotion for the Bournemouth firemen at a standstill. This situation could have been changed by the senior firemen at Bournemouth. To explain briefly, if a fireman secured a driver's job at another depot with a request to return to his home depot when his seniority 'came up', no driver regardless of his age or seniority could fill a vacancy at that fireman's home depot until that fireman had returned as a driver unless he was redundant. This meant that all the firemen who were senior to the man who had moved away were assured of getting their drivers' jobs at their depot before this man could move back.

So I started to pay more attention to the vacancy sheet that was posted at all depots every two months. I took note of vacancies that I had a chance of filling and the first was a vacancy at St Leonards. I applied for it even though I had no idea where it was but I was unlucky.

I wasn't very disappointed but it brought home to me that it wasn't going to be as simple as all that to get a driver's job. Firemen at many other depots were also looking for vacancies and it was just a matter of being patient. Even a fireman with only one day's seniority would secure promotion before I did.

Meanwhile it was back to my firing career. Some turns of duty were anticipated more than others. One of my favourites involved working the 18.45 from Bournemouth all stations to Basingstoke, getting relieved and relieving on the Nine Elms goods to Southampton East Docks, getting relieved again and relieving the 'Cockneys' who had passed us with the Channel Isles boat train somewhere between Basingstoke and Worting. We then worked the Mail train from Southampton Terminus back to Bournemouth.

This involved three different firing techniques. First the stopping train puff-puffing to the next distant signal, shutting off, fill the boiler up, stop at the station, shut off the injector and puff-puff to the next distant, the same routine from station to station, interlaced with a few shovelfuls of coal, not too heavy but just enough to keep a steady hot fire. Then the heavy goods, slow, powerful with the engine giving her all. And lastly the Mail train flashing through the New Forest to home.

It is however the Goods train that I am going to try to bring to life once again. I never tired of that part of the turn.

We would wait on the down local platform at

33. Dear old 548, she must rate as the old maid of Bournemouth and as unpredictable as any woman. One day she would burn her fire bright and steam freely, the next day her fire would have to be coaxed and she would turn her nose up. I always felt that a smaller chimney to give her a sharper blast would have made a big difference (I believe that her sister, 549, did in fact work from Norwood Junction with a stovepipe chimney). However, 548 proved herself when called upon to work to Waterloo, as if she relished the chance to stretch her legs, and more than surprised both my driver, Joe Langdon, and myself.

33. R. A. Panting

Basingstoke while the Basingstoke crew slowly drew into the platform and stopped for water. I would scramble over the tender to put the water pipe in, exchanging a few words with the Basingstoke crew.

'65 on mate, ten vacuums.'

'What's she like?'

'Not much good, dirty tube plate.'

As soon as the tender was full of water we would be away. By now the safety valves would be blowing slightly and the driver would slowly ease her away from the platform. Getting all the loose couplings tight, he would pull the lever up and break the regulator open into the second regulator valve. I would wait for the blast to brighten the fire, spending my time adjusting the lubricator or, if the rail was wet, working the sanding lever. With the engine getting into her stride I would put up the half-door and feed the Nine Elms hard black over the top. With the glow from the firebox throwing up on to the plume of smoke and steam that billowed back and over the cab I would put on the injector, cutting it down as fine as it would go. I didn't want too much water in the boiler as we turned the top of the bank at Litchfield – we would be coasting into Southampton Terminus from there and the boiler would have to be kept quiet.

As we blasted away from Basingstoke this would be the steam engine at its best, a heavy load, every beat a full blast up the chimney, four blasts to the wheel each distinguishable from the next, each blast thrusting the boiler into the darkness ahead.

Looking back over the wagons, a plume of steam would be visible against the lights of Basingstoke. This would be the Elms men on the Channel Isle boat train fast overtaking us on the down main. With many 'rockets' being thrown up into the night sky they would steam by us with a rude blast on their whistle, both the crew shouting good-humoured remarks as the footplates passed, the glow from their fire lighting up grinning faces. But watch out – they might just empty the grouts from their tea-can over you. Then they would be gone, the lighted carriages passing us at ever-increasing speed to leave us again in our own little world.

My driver would have eased our engine down slightly to give the boat train a chance to clear Worting Junction; they had to clear Worting before we would get the all clear.

Worting home signal would come into view over the trees, showing green. The boat train would now be well on her way to Micheldever and this would be the signal to open our engine right up, this time she would not be held back. Slowly the beat would quicken and grow more quiet as the lever was wound back towards 40 per cent cut off, a little bit at a time. As the blast threw the smoke and steam up into the night sky I would keep the steady flow of coal over the half-door, feet astride swinging from left to right, so easy, so wonderful, the ring of the shovel on the fire door, the injector singing softly, the safety valves humming slightly with a full head of steam, the heat, the smell, the crescendo of noise that is the steam engine echoing back from the night stillness of the trees and banks. How wonderful to be an engineman on engines like these. Built before my time, fired to and driven by hundreds of different men, abused and thrashed, and treated well by good enginemen. My grandfather had fired to and driven these, and now they were performing for me. These were real engines that would give of their best as long as life was breathed into them with fire and water.

Topping the bank, the driver would shut off steam and coast on the brake down through Popham, Micheldever, Winchester and Eastleigh into Southampton Terminus. Slowly threading our way over the points into the terminus docks road we would come to a stand at

Canute Road crossing for relief by Eastleigh men. A walk across to the Terminus Loco then we relieved the Nine Elms men who had passed us out of Basingstoke, a few words and sarcastic humour jokingly thrown from both sides, their boat train engine waiting for us, having been turned and watered for our final dash back to Bournemouth and bed.

34. Urie S15 no. 30509 at Basingstoke with a Nine Elms to Southampton Docks freight train. The fireman has taken the time to have the duty number pasted on the headboard. This is typical of the class of train and engine we would work out of Basingstoke at night. I don't remember ever coming up against a bad engine of this class, and it was a very good freight engine. That tall chimney emphasised the magic of a steam engine – work this engine hard out of Basingstoke and she would respond with a low drone from the safety valves as the steam pressure held on maximum. That low drone was a peculiarity of these engines and on a clear frosty night would carry for miles. Note the massive balance weight in the driving wheel.

Next time you listen to recordings of locomotives, because this is now all we have left, disregard the 'Atlantic Coast Express' or whatever you have rushing through Basingstoke, the whole character of the leading lady lost in an explosion of noise and clatter, and listen to the goods engine, turn the volume up loud and fill the room with that wonderful steady beat.

The March, May and July vacancy sheets of 1958 were posted and on each sheet there were vacancies at, of all places, Brighton. Now I had never before given Brighton a thought. Hopefully I applied each month and as my seniority was greater than that of the senior unappointed man at Brighton I felt sure that I would be successful. I even took a trip to Brighton depot to look over the place and see the sort of work involved, but this was where fate stepped in on my railway career. Men who previously had no intentions of leaving their beloved Devon found themselves redundant and being forced either to move to fresh depots or to leave the job. Like all of us who knew nothing but railway work, railway firemen were no good outside the railway. So these were the men who filled the Brighton vacancies as fast as they became available. I don't expect they were very popular with the Sussex men; to work twelve years or more at a depot as a fireman and then see the drivers' jobs being filled by outsiders really hurt. Nothing illegal was being done as such moves were in accordance with the Promotion, Transfer and Redundancy Arrangements as agreed between the unions and the management.

Through the summer of 1958 I continued my firing career at Bournemouth, taking my turns on the main line along with the other turns involved in number two link. I wasn't complaining, I still had the best engineman at Bournemouth to fire to, and Joe and I worked together with an understanding that had reached perfection over the miles and months that we had been together. I knew Joe's every move by heart, just where he would shut off steam or pull the lever up into a shorter cut-off, where he expected a full head of steam and where he expected the engine to keep quiet. Coupled with the fact that the general condition of the engines had greatly improved, mainly due to the introduction of the many rebuilt Pacifics, my job was now as easy as it could ever be. Indeed it made a pleasant change to get a rough engine now and again if only to prove to myself that I could still master it. It also gave Joe great delight to see me sweating and swearing.

One Sunday during the summer of 1958 Joe and I were booked to work a return excursion to Waterloo. I remember threading my way through the crowds on the up platform, following Joe. We waited at the end of the platform for our train to come steaming round from the West, and when she finally appeared we had the shock of our lives, for heading ten bogies was old 30548. Bournemouth had two of these Qs: '48 and '49. They were used solely for goods work and travelling shunters, or filling in on three-coach school trains or parcel trains. A one-stop to Waterloo, never.

Joe swung up on to the footplate, his Devonshire accent really coming out as it did when he was roused. 'What this, then?'

'It's the only engine they've got, Joe,' replied the driver. 'Your engine fell down with brick arch trouble and this is the biggest engine in steam. The running foreman said that you can stop at Eastleigh and change engines if you want to.'

I was still getting over the shock and surveyed the situation with my heart in my boots. I didn't mind a challenge on a rough Pacific or Nelson, at least they were man enough for the job even if steam wasn't plentiful, but this was ridiculous.

I glanced over the boiler front, nicely wiped down and clean, a full head of steam and a glass full of water, plenty of heat against my legs from the half-open fire door, the blower cracked open just enough to keep the smoke down and the tender well stacked up with good coal: altogether a very good preparation. The fireman I'd relieved was making his getaway with a rather-you-than-me look on his face. The driver made his departure saying, 'I made sure the fire was clean before it was made up, Jim.'

As for Joe, he said, 'We'll get to Southampton, Jacky, and ask for another engine from there.' We had no alternative, knowing the engine was just about good enough to get us to Southampton, a short non-stop run.

At the signal from the guard we set off. I remember shutting the fire door and letting the blast do its work to liven up the fire, and by the time that Joe shut off steam at Pokesdown to run down Christchurch bank, half a glass of water was gone already. I turned the blower on hard. Now the fire was hot I didn't want it to settle down on the bars, and I put both injectors on to fill the boiler up for the climb out of Christchurch. Being a comparatively small boiler it soon filled to the top of the glass and, knowing how these engines were prone to priming when worked hard, I reckoned this was plenty. Running through Christchurch with the injectors turned off she made her full head of steam. Now everything was full and hot where it should be, everything in our favour so far, but we still had an awful lot of hard work ahead of us.

Joe put the lever into 35 per cent cut-off and lifted the regulator to the roof. Now 35 on these engines could mean anything between 25 and 45; there was so much play between the die-block, the reversing links and the numerous pins that the pointer on the lever would never hold still, and the harder the engine was worked the more the lever leapt back and forth, the only guide being the roar from the chimney. Regardless of this, Joe worked the engine hard by his normal

standards but being the driver he was, he knew to what limits he could stretch it.

Opening the fire door revealed the fire up under the ring of the door and sloping sharply down to a white-hot front. With the sloping firebox on this type of engine this was ideal. I took time to lift the end of the baffle plate with the firing shovel to look at the tube plate. It was clean with a whiteness round the tubes that was a sign of good coal and good combustion. This whiteness was very fine and could be found around the firebox door on any engine when using good coal properly, and I can remember years ago an old driver wiping it off the door with his cloth and polishing the brass work with it.

I started firing, keeping the coal up under the baffle plate. Two or three quick shovelfuls and slam the door shut, break up the coal on the shovelling plate, open up and two or three more, break up the next lot of coal and dispose of that. The engine responded by lifting her safety valves, and I quickly put the driver's injector on, not bothering to cut it down fine as the small delivery of these injectors would hold the water level. We topped the bank and headed for New Milton with the needle right on the mark and two-thirds of a glass of water. Joe kept the settings as they were and I kept up the steady firing. I've never known that engine steam like that before or since.

At the top of Sway bank Joe shut off for the run through Brockenhurst, on with the blower again to keep her hot and the chance now to put my injector on as well to give the coal a good dampening down and to recover that precious inch of water that I'd lost. Shutting off my injector before clattering through Brockenhurst and easing the driver's injector down now as fine as I could get it, I knew that the final dash to Southampton would be easy providing I did my part. I would not shut the injector off again, knowing

57

that she would steam against it. This typifies how you had to keep one jump ahead of the engine because once she got on top you would be in for a rough run.

So we ran into Southampton and Joe out of force of habit stopped the engine right for water. Looking at his watch, he said, 'Well, she did that all right, Jacky. Only a minute down.' The tone of his voice telling me that he was thinking the

same as I was, it came as no surprise when he said, 'How about it, shall we take her through? We're allowed ten minutes more than the normal service.' I said, 'Why not, Joe? Let's try it.'

We got the right away from the station staff and we were off on the last lap, a long one but the last one.

Once again I let her fire get hot and treated her the same as I had from Bournemouth, and once again she responded. We passed through Eastleigh with the needle right over and the injector singing away. There was no stopping now, she was going to punch her way up to Waltham block post before I could have a breather. So I busied myself, firing steadily and checking the lubricator sight feeds, checking the distant signals, brushing up, dampening down, swinging the shovel. Slam the door open and shut, pull

35. No. 30770, 'Sir Prianius', was the last King Arthur left in service. Here she is at the end, completely out of character on a docks freight train passing Worting Junction, or Battledown as I like to call it. This was Battledown Junction before the flyover was built. Pushing her way up towards the top of the bank, a King Arthur would have to be worked harder with her big driving wheels as compared to the smaller-wheeled S15 class. The steam chest pressure would be so high that sometimes it would be impossible to get the exhaust injector to work, and the fireman would have to use the driver's live steam injector.

35. G. R. Siviour

down the coal, break the lumps, it was all happening. We reached the top of the bank and at last Joe could ease her down a little for the run to his shutting-off point, bridge number 148, the one with the gate in the middle.

Reaching this, he closed the regulator and we took stock. We'd lost half a glass of water but we would get this back running to Worting Junction. Joe checked his watch and we were on time. I remembered a driver saying in the drivers' room once, 'To time a train up the bank you only needed to average 43 miles per hour.' And as we were allowed an extra ten minutes with this train between Southampton and Waterloo it was feasible that we had in fact run to time.

Passing over the flyover at Worting junction, Joe opened her up again for the dash through Basingstoke and on to Waterloo. On the gently falling gradients that we were now to encounter on the run in she started to gain speed, and with the train pushing up the tender we reached speeds that this engine was not built for. The tender started to vibrate against the engine due to the slack draw-bar between them. This resulted in all the coal from the tender being shaken forward on to the footplate, and not only that but the carefully built fire was now being shaken down to the front of the firebox, exposing the back corners. This was no good for this engine, she wanted a fire up under the door, not under the brick arch. I got the pricker down from the tender and frantically tried to pull the fire back, but at the same time I was still having to replenish the fire that was being shaken through the bars and blasted out of the chimney.

I fought for every ounce of steam, sprinkled the coal lightly, pulled the fire back with the pricker, sprinkled some more, working the door for each shovelful. I couldn't let any heat sneak out of the door. I wanted it all through the tubes. I couldn't afford to allow too much air into the top of the fire, even though auxiliary air through the door would help a good combustion. I wanted all the air to be drawn up through the grate to keep the fire hot.

Anyway, with Joe using his knowledge of the gradients to help me we struggled on. Now I had to watch the water – every time I worked the injector I dared not waste a drop. This was also Joe's concern. The only water column was at Walton-on-Thames on the through; there was one at Woking on the slow road but this would mean stopping and advising the signalman at Woking. I knew from experience that this caused unbelievable disruption. So Walton-on-Thames would be our obvious choice, and it was the last column on the main line before Waterloo.

Through Woking it was obvious by the green signals that we were behind time – any other time we could guarantee being checked and even stopped. What a blessing this would have been now, but we had greens all the way until approaching Byfleet junction, and what a beautiful sight, there was his semaphore distant showing caution. Joe shut off steam and opened the blower, I in turn increased the injectors. We now had to get back all we could. As Joe slowed for the stop signal I waited till our speed had dropped to a crawl and nipped up over the coal. Dropping the pricker into the tender, I found we had over a foot of water left. Joe agreed that this would see us through and that there was no need to lose any more time taking water.

With that the signal was pulled off (he must have been crossing something over at Weybridge) but this respite was all we needed. The boiler was nearly full and the needle was leaning over the right way. So with no more checks we picked up speed again and went through to Waterloo, showing no sign of the struggle we had had, apart from our black faces and the dust that covered everything.

We had in fact lost ten minutes from Worting,

but our gain was far greater. The satisfaction that I secretly felt was echoed in Joe's voice as he closed the vacuum ejector. 'Well, we got here, Jacky.'

As I filled the bucket to wash, to clean up, our cockney relief showed up. 'Where'd you get this one from? Woking yard?'

'No,' I replied, 'we've worked her through from Bournemouth,' I knew from the look on his face that he didn't believe me.

The summer workings of 1958 ended and I was no nearer securing a driver's appointment. I had decided to hold back future applications until movements from the west country ceased, as they must eventually do so.

I was booked one day with a driver in the top link, up with the 9.30 and back with the Belle. This driver was one of those who considered himself one of God's chosen few, always looking for points to pull his firemen up over, always free with his criticism of firemen regardless of how well they performed their work. If he had a rough trip it was always the fireman's fault, never the engine's.

We were on our way back after a good trip up, and I'd been on my best behaviour making sure that he would have nothing to complain about. Now one of the fireman's duties was to observe the distant signals. This was all part of keeping control of the boiler, for if a signal was at caution, you were ready to open the injectors to keep the boiler pressure down and thus prevent blowing off steam. Some distant signals the fireman saw before the driver, and the routine that I had was to throw out my left arm and shout 'Right so-and-so distant'.

We steamed through Brockenhurst and I had the fire just right for the run into Bournemouth. Checking Lymington junction distant first, I then busied myself tidying up the footplate ready for my relief. Climbing up Sway bank, I shut the tender coal-hole and washed down the footplate, filled the bucket with water and prepared to wash up, silently congratulating myself that the trip had been uneventful and the driver wasn't going to have anything to complain about. This had been an excellent trip.

Topping the bank, I peered under the bridge to see Sway distant. It was in the all clear position, so I yelled out, 'Right Sway distant', and started to get washed up.

The driver came over, tapped me on the shoulder and said, 'What's up with you, don't you think I know the road?'

I was too taken back to reply – even carrying out my job to the letter was wrong.

Another incident concerning this driver happened to another fireman. They were climbing the bank between Winchester and Micheldever with the up Birkenhead. They had a King Arthur pressed at 200 lb. boiler pressure. He had everything just right, the injector singing away maintaining the boiler level and the boiler steam gauge hanging on 190 lb. Ideal, one would think, but no, this driver looked at his watch passing Weston, came over to the fireman, pointed to the steam gauge and shouted, 'Get that other ten pound of steam, we're losing time.'

How could anyone win with a driver like that?

November 1958 was the turning point in my career. Joe and I had worked a train up to Waterloo and were waiting for our relief. Up on the footplate climbed two youngsters, both looking like they'd just left school. This was our relief.

Joe asked, 'Which one of you is the driver then?'

'I am, mate,' said one of them.

To say that Joe and I were taken back would put it mildly. It seemed only a few weeks ago that this chap was helping me turn my engines round on Nine Elms pit, and here he was now relieving my driver. This got home to me more than anything that I was fast missing the boat. All the way back I dwelt on this and made up my mind then that when I got back to Bournemouth depot, the November vacancy sheet having just been posted, I was going to put in for a driver's job regardless, regardless of where it was as long as it was at a good depot. Arriving back I scanned the vacancy sheet, seeing the usual jobs at suburban electric depots, jobs that were advertised time and time again. These were no good to me, they were convenient for firemen with little service who were eager to get in the grade of driver. I had the seniority to be a bit choosy.

Two depots that had vacancies appealed to me – there were two jobs at Nine Elms and three at Stewarts Lane, so it was between the Elms and the Lane.

Giving it a little thought I decided that if I was going to make the break I was going to do it properly. I was going to find out what another railway was like.

36. Bulleid Q1 no. 33020 running down Ringwood bank with a freight from Brockenhurst. The 'Charlies' were not everybody's cup of tea; you either liked them or hated them. With a boiler pressure of 230 lb. and those small driving wheels they were very strong, and providing they had the steam they were more than capable of the work that Mr Bulleid designed them for, heavy wartime trains. Built as an austerity engine, they had an intended life of ten years but far exceeded this. No. 33020 had a mechanical lubricator for the steam chest mounted on the front framing, just visible above the front buffer. Earlier numbers had a hydrostatic lubricator mounted in the cab that every fireman had clouted his head on at some time.

5
The Other Railway

Whilst I was awaiting the results of the vacancy sheet to be published it became known at the Bournemouth depot that 'Evans has put in for a job at Stewarts Lane'. I had kept it to myself, but nothing is ever confidential on the railway. Too many people are involved. One driver informed me that he'd spent more time in one link than I had on the railway. I told him straight that that was his fault, not mine. Others didn't hesitate to inform me that I had to 'pass' yet. This meant I had yet to pass the driving exam. Such was the confidence they gave me. These drivers seemed to object to the fact that I, a fireman, was going to become a driver. Of course there were other drivers who wished me luck, some of them digging to the back of their lockers and coming up with instruction books of all descriptions. Some of these drivers surprised me with their sudden interest in me, indeed this was a side of them that had never been evident all the time I had known them.

Two weeks later the result of the vacancy sheet was posted, and as was expected I had secured one of the jobs at the 'Lane', to quote the wording, 'Subject to qualifying'. This meant subject to passing the driver's exam. The exam had been changed since the last Bournemouth fireman had had to undergo this terrifying experience: whereas it had always been a written exam, it was now oral. This was something that no fireman looked forward to, but something we all had to do eventually. Years ago, though, a fireman could opt to refuse to take the exam when his turn came, but he then had to accept a fireman's job in a non-promotional link for the rest of his days. I believe that at the time of my firing days there was one such fireman at Southampton Docks, who retired as a fireman.

I was going to have to sit across the table from the inspector and answer questions as they were put to me one day, and take a train on a journey with the inspector riding on the footplate the next day. If a fireman failed the first time he went in again after three months. If still unsuccessful he had a third attempt after six months, and if he failed this third time he then had to give up the footplate and take a job in the shed, as a rule that of steam raiser.

I asked when I could expect to meet the inspector and was told that it would be whenever the inspector had the time. Typically, no one was worried that I was eager to take my place at Stewarts Lane except myself. I was going to have to wait for the wheels of officialdom to turn in their own good time. Meanwhile this would give me time to learn all I could, remembering what one driver used to tell me:

'One day you'll be outside the depot as a driver and then you're on your own, you have to answer to everything.' This was only too true, it was always the driver who had to reply to reports, lost time, mishaps, bad steaming etc. Realising this, I had a lot of learning to do in a very short time.

It was seven weeks of swotting, sweating and studying before I was notified that the next day I was to appear before the footplate inspector. This was in the first week of the new year, 1959. So at eight o'clock in the morning of the appointed day I presented myself at the mutual instruction classroom, clutching my rule book complete with all amendments, trimming wire, worsted and pliers and a pen.

I had expected the local inspector, who passed

37. N class no. 31403 on one of the disposal pits at Stewarts Lane. The fireman's hand on the clinker shovel can be seen as he ladles out the clinker and dirt. Much overtime could be made on the pit at the Lane, such was the turnaround of engines. There would always be more engines waiting to have their fires cleaned and to be prepared for leaving shed on another duty. When I arrived at the Lane the Pacifics were more in evidence and the pits would be continually full of dropped fires and ashes, making it impossible to rake out the ashpans on the more orthodox engines. These engines would leave shed with ashpans still full, and with this class of engine, once she started 'bouncing' along, the crew would soon be made aware of the conditions as they became covered in a fine white dust.

all Bournemouth men, and was surprised when Mr Baden Pope of Basingstoke turned up. He will be remembered for his very good articles on the steam engine that appeared regularly in the *Locomotive Journal*. Here was one of the few men

63

who knew all the answers. I only hoped I did.

As I followed him into the room it dawned on me why I was not sitting before our own inspector: we both had the same name, J. Evans. Did the powers up top really notice such things? Even though we were not related, I assume they must, as I had never known anyone but the local inspector 'pass' Bournemouth men.

I was to face forty-two questions on the engine and twenty on the rule book. It crossed my mind at the time that before, men had gone in to pass in twos – would he ask me every alternate question as would be the case if I had a partner? No such luck. He started with the engine questions and we slowly plodded through the complete paper. Preparation of the engine, boiler construction, firebox construction, reason for the brick arch, the reasons for bad steaming, injectors exhaust and live steam, the difference between fixed and moving cone

38. No. 30769, 'Sir Balan', passing through St Mary Cray junction on 16 May 1959, just prior to the South Eastern Electrification Scheme, phase one. The road here being used was the old down fast; later these roads were altered to read from the left, instead of two up and two down, up local, down local, up fast, down fast. The new-look crossovers can be appreciated here, as long as ten bogies to allow the new electric trains to cross from one line to another with hardly a falter. The old, short crossovers had been a saviour more than once for the steam engine, the fireman breathing a sigh of relief as his driver shut off the demand for steam to negotiate the tighter curves.

38. S. C. Nash

injectors, vacuum ejectors and brakes and reasons for failing, Westinghouse brakes and triple valves, testing and changing gauge glasses, packing regulators and the working of the regulator valves, Superheater header and tubes.

39. One of the LMS 2–6–4Ts shedded at Stewarts Lane, no. 42088, having her tubes blown out under the viaducts at Stewarts Lane. In my opinion, using compressed air for this job was not as efficient as the old way of twisting a short length of whistle wire around the end of a tube rod and splaying the ends out. This would scour out the insides of the tubes and remove the hard scale – a job that would be reluctantly carried out at Bournemouth on the foreman's instructions by any fireman who happened to be spare. It was not a very pleasant job at the best of times, and obviously not part of the Stewarts Lane fireman's curriculum.

39. John Ashman FRPS

Name the Walschaert and Stephenson valve gear and motion, the method for disconnecting an engine for a broken piston, connecting rod, big end bolts, coupling rods and valve linkages. Hydrostatic and mechanical lubricators and finally finishing up in time for dinner with my making plug and tail trimmings, having to explain what parts of the engine they were for, and how to increase or decrease the flow of oil.

As I walked across to the station buffet for a well-earned cup of tea, I contemplated that so far it hadn't been too bad. There had been no catch questions and the only one that I'd had trouble over was a very simple one, a question that had two answers, a technical and an easy answer. I gave him the technical one, when in fact the answer he wanted for the paper was the easy one.

About 2 pm we continued with the second paper, twenty questions on the rules. Once again every question was straightforward, covering every aspect of the rules governing footplate work. Starting with the old favourite, rule 55, and progressing through passing signals at danger, failure of automatic signals and telephones, tablet and staff and ticket working and failures with same, single-line working over a double road with a pilotman and once again failures, and failures using the four wrong line order forms, protection of the train and other running lines for a derailment, fire, and failure of engine.

By four o'clock we had finished, and as Inspector Pope put away the papers he told me that I was all right, and he would see me tomorrow for the practical examination. He said that he would be watching out for control and working of the engine, braking when running in stations and, surprise surprise, control of the fireman as in the case of excessive smoke, steam or dust. As he said, 'Don't be afraid to tell him, that is all part of your job.'

The next day he arrived with the 05.40 from

Waterloo, and we climbed aboard the engine to work the 09.00 to Weymouth. Even though he was an inspector, he still had to ask the Weymouth driver, 'I'm passing this fireman for driver. Can I have your engine?'

The driver agreed but I noticed the look of reluctance as he got off the seat of the King Arthur – even though he'd been driving for years he still enjoyed swinging open the regulator and feeling the engine pound away, such was the great attraction of the steam engine.

I worked down to Weymouth and worked a return back to Bournemouth. I remained standing because this was how I felt the job should be done, on my feet and alert, and so much depended on how I performed these duties. Arriving back at Bournemouth we stood on the platform and Inspector Pope said, 'Well, that's it, son. You're OK. Best of luck with your medical.' He shook my hand and that was it: subject to passing the medical I was now a driver.

A few days later I was sent to Eastleigh to report to the company doctor and was pronounced fit for the duties of engine driver. It now remained for me to be transferred to Stewarts Lane, but I was going to have to wait yet again. Something to do with the rosters at Stewarts Lane with regard to the rotation of rest day workings, so I was told. After waiting a couple of weeks I went into the office at Bournemouth intent on getting an explanation why I had not yet been transferred, and if they were not yet transferring me why I could not be put on driving duties at Bournemouth. I was informed that I was a driver at Stewarts Lane not at Bournemouth and as such I could not drive at Bournemouth but would be expected to continue on the fireman's roster until Stewarts Lane was ready to accept me. So I still had to continue firing and accept the fact that there was not much I could do about it. I got fed up explaining to enquiries why I was still at Bournemouth, and 'I

thought you had a driver's job'. At least I could perform my job with a certain amount of light-heartedness, happy in the knowledge that the one thing that firemen worried about was behind me, the ordeal of 'passing out'.

At last, at the beginning of February I was notified that on the following Monday I would be transferred to Stewarts Lane and would be expected to report to the shedmaster in the morning of the said day.

It was only then that I started to have qualms about what I'd let myself in for. Here I was, moving away from Bournemouth and a good position in the links, one of the best paid links with plenty of well paid mileage, to a junior driver's position with junior driver's money and no mileage allowance. A top fireman's weekly basic was nine pounds ten shillings (£9.50), a first year driver's pay was ten pounds four shillings (£10.20), so I was moving for a rise of fourteen shillings (70p) a week without the extras that I had enjoyed these last few years. It took six years of gradual rises to get to the top driver's rate of eleven pounds eleven shillings (£11.55).

Whether I'd done right or not the choice had been mine and mine only and I was going to have to make the best of it. After all, I reasoned, other men moved away to drivers' jobs and they managed all right. If they could make out, so could I. I admit, though, to being a little worried. I'd been at Bournemouth so long I was part of it and to work at another depot, a complete stranger, made me feel I was moving to the other side of the world.

My last Saturday at Bournemouth depot passed and I cleared out my locker, passing round to other firemen my valued books. I wouldn't need those again. I was wished the best of luck by a few, whilst others were more concerned with the move up in the roster. Was I sorry? Of course I was. I enjoyed my firing, pitting myself against the engine, but now it was

40. One of the Stewarts Lane's E1 4–4–0s, no. 31506, leaving Victoria Eastern with a Kent Coast train. An empty train carrying this head code would be heading for Eardly sidings. The South Eastern drivers spoke highly of these, their own engines. The Paris sleeper, the 'Blue', might have one of this class double-heading a Merchant Navy. With my experience of Merchants I found it hard to believe that Shepherd's Well or Sole Street banks would have proved too much with this train, without the assistance of a 4–4–0. On the little work I did with them I found them more than capable, providing once again that the steam was available.

all over. I felt like those old drivers that I had seen through the years walking away for the last time with their grub bag under their arm.

As I was off duty on the Sunday I went up to Eastleigh to see my grandfather. I had not so far told him of my promotion in case I failed to 'pass', but he greeted my news with a 'Well done, my bonny'. We now had a third-generation engine driver, and I think he was more pleased than I was. As for Stewarts Lane, he said, 'That depot has its own laws, but it's a good depot.' How very right he was.

Arriving at Waterloo I made my way to my digs to deposit my case and then tried to find my way into Stewarts Lane loco. I walked down, eventually finding myself under the South Western bridge, having passed the Dewdrop where years ago my grandmother used to go for her pint of 'porter', and the terraced house where she and grandfather lived when he was a fireman at Nine Elms. Crossing the footbridge over the running lines I looked down upon a scene that I shall never forget. There were engines everywhere, all belching smoke and steam, a sea of chimneys, safety valves and whistles, such activity as I had never seen before. After the sedate order at Bournemouth, with the strict observance of boiler control, I began to wonder what I had let myself in for.

Having reported to Mr Inge, the shedmaster, I made myself known to the roster clerk. He informed me that I would be taking the vacancy in the Eastern dual link until such time as my seniority took me to a vacancy at Victoria East-ern. I would be booked 08.00 to 16.00 every day, including rest days, to learn roads and signals. Sundays I would be booked in as ordered for preparation and disposal duties. This was wel-come news, as working rest days would give me an extra twelve hours a week, worth more than two Bournemouth to Waterloo trips, and there would be no shortage of Sundays, worth four-teen hours a time.

For three weeks I rode around on engines and electric trains, concentrating on the lines applic-able to the dual link. Victoria to Orpington,

Holborn Viaduct to Sevenoaks and Wimbledon and the Catford loop. Herne Hill and Eardly sidings and Kensington, and that was about it. The range of the dual link that I was in was very limited, and this was going to restrict me for other work, but I was going to find this out later on.

After the three weeks I was booked to attend the electric school to be trained as a motorman. There were nine drivers from the Lane and three from the Elms and the course would take three weeks. I was going to have to learn about a completely different form of traction to satisfy the inspector.

The training and passing out ordeal behind me, I returned once again to road-learning during the week and pit relief on Sundays. The weeks dragged by, road-learning was very tedious, but Sundays I looked forward to. Not only because it gave me the chance to work on steam engines, types of engines that I'd never seen before or even knew existed, but also this was another chance to get to know the men. Waiting in the cabin for the next job and being able to make up a four at cards really broke the ice. Wherever footplate men wait as ordered or spare, you will find a card school, and the training I'd had at Bournemouth stood me in good stead. It was only now that my colleagues started to associate me with the new name on the roster.

The drivers' cabin or, as the South Eastern called it, drivers' lobby, at the Lane is worth a mention. I had been in many cabins but this one took some beating. It was about fifteen feet wide and about fifty feet long, with the table and forms bolted to the floor right down the middle. Cleanliness was non-existent, the whole being nothing but a big black cavern. Some obscure person would now and again push a broom round in an effort to clear the accumulation of old sandwiches, cigarette packets and other articles that were thrown on the floor – a practice, I'm sorry to say, that was rife in drivers' cabins, although I found that the smaller depots made some attempt to keep the cabin clean. It was a case of the bigger the depot the worse it was, and at Stewarts Lane, with the coming and going of so many men, it was really bad.

After a few weeks of this rather menial routine I was called into the office and asked to sign my route knowledge card. As I knew enough routes for the Eastern dual link I would now work my rostered turns. One benefit I was going to gain from having to work around the clock was the opportunity when on nights to get home during the day to my family, catching the first train down in the morning and the last train back at night. For this reason I would change turns within my link and work as many nights as possible. I could then use the free pass that was part of my promotion conditions to get home from Friday to Tuesday.

Now I was in my own link it gave me the chance to work some of the overtime that was always available. Even returning after completing a full day's work, there was always a pit full of engines waiting to be disposed of and it was only a case of telling the foreman, who was very willing to get another engine off the pit and prepared, ready to go again.

Another thing that was so different from Bournemouth, and something that I found very strange, was that there was no such thing as 'senior men, senior work'. If there was an extra boat train to Dover or Folkestone or a passenger

41. Schools class no. 30915, 'Brighton', taking water at the Central section side of Victoria. Note the length of the water crane, which must have been the longest on British Rail! This engine would work out of Victoria, getting a hefty push along the platform by the station pilot, and with plenty of regulator and lever, pound up over Grosvenor bridge to cross the Thames and sweep down through Clapham Junction to achieve the magical 'Balham in nine'. This was akin to the South Western's 'Hampton Court in eighteen'.

42. Stewarts Lane on 3 June 1961. What a different scene to how it used to be when I first saw it as a mass of smoking chimneys and protesting safety valves. The running foreman sat in the middle of the lot in his wartime reinforced cabin, with engine sheets before him, issuing his orders to the two 'runners' who in turn directed the engine crews on the marshalling of engines. Note the remaining evidence of what was a South Eastern practice, and would never have been allowed at Bournemouth, that of shovelling the small coal over the side when making up a fire. Every water column had this tell-tale pile, but it did serve as a good marker for setting an engine right for water.

to Ramsgate the nearest driver to the turn worked it regardless of his seniority, and if no driver was available then a passed man worked the turn. Even a fireman of twenty-three, just passed for driving, would get the same chance for main line driving. What a difference from Bournemouth, where to cover one main line turn would involve two, three or even four alterations. The rule at Stewarts Lane was that a driver is a driver, likewise a fireman is a fireman, no matter what their seniority.

I didn't have the chance to learn the main line beyond Swanley and Sevenoaks in one direction or Dartford in the other, so I had no chance to drive any main line trains. My sole experience with steam engines in my new capacity as a driver, apart from disposing and oiling, consisted of shunting at Herne Hill sorting sidings and Victoria, parcel trains from Holborn to Victoria, milk trains to Kensington, the occasional excursion to New Cross ballast sidings and empty trains to and from Eardly sidings. Passing over the Bournemouth main line at Queens Road, I would look enviously at the Pacifics dashing up and down, having to resign myself that my sole experience with these engines was going to be no more than light engine running between Stewarts Lane and Victoria. I was never going to get the chance to open a Pacific regulator in earnest.

My colleagues frequently reminded me that I had come from a 'billiard top' railway as they termed it, and another favourite topic was when the South Eastern was loaned Drummond T9's. I forget the reason for this, but I do know that the South Eastern men were not very impressed, my favourite punch-line being that these engines were built for firemen not navvies. Things that I had taken for granted were pointed out to me, one being the fact that these engines rarely failed to slip getting away, regardless of the condition of the rail. Another was the dry sand and the fact that the fireman had to work the lever back and forth to shake the sand down the pipe. Then the reverser would not reverse with a full steam chest, the driver having to bend to drag the cylinder cocks lever up from off the floor of the footplate before the steam reverser would oblige. And why was the firehole door so low down and the firebox devoid of any slope? I began to wonder how the South Western men had done such good work on the main line with an engine with so many faults, remembering that it was only a short while back that Dorchester men were working the down Mail from Southampton Terminus to Weymouth with ten bogies with those engines. In all fairness to my new colleagues, though, they had their share of hard work. The rounders, a circular trip via the coast road with passenger service trains and stoppers from Ramsgate, would not have been easy going.

In January 1960 I at last obtained accommodation for my family in London. The worry of finding somewhere to live deterred many family men from taking the step up from the home counties, though the railway authorities were most helpful in more ways than one in assisting men such as myself to find a home in the metropolis. Having arranged my removal, paid for by the railway because mine was a promotional move, I loaded the car with my family including the goldfish, budgerigar and cat, and left Bournemouth.

So we arrived in Streatham SW16. What a treat after nearly a year, being able to leave home and get to work in less than fifteen minutes, but I would soon be moving to Victoria – it was only a matter of time. By this time the new Stewarts Lane electric depot had opened with the consequent transferring of drivers from the dual links. Phase one of the South Eastern electrification scheme was now operative, the new trains working to Ramsgate and Dover via Faversham. The amount of work being lost by the steam depot was quite noticeable. This was the start of the end of Stewarts Lane, although steam engines were still working to the channel ports via Tonbridge, and shunting engines were still required. The air of gloom hung over the whole depot, and engines were put down the ends of the shed having reached the end of their days. But somehow there still seemed to be plenty of work to do, as the manning of the depot was being run down at the same time.

Some Pacifics were sent over to Nine Elms, presumably to replace the King Arthurs at that depot, and I believe Bricklayers Arms still retained a certain amount of work out of Charing Cross and Cannon Street.

6
Main Line Driver

It was not until March 1961 that I was notified that I would be transferred to Victoria Eastern. I had been at the Lane two years and two months and was sorry to have to change depots once again, but regardless of how I felt I realised that electric traction was of the prime importance.

Arriving at my new depot, I was given a few weeks to learn the roads that I needed to know in relation to the work at the depot. This involved the road beyond Swanley to Ramsgate, Otford to Maidstone and roads to Rochester via Dartford, and Dover Marine via Faversham. Phase two of the electrification was now in progress, laying the third rail from Orpington and Ramsgate down to Folkestone and Dover, likewise from Minster to Ashford and Maidstone to Ashford. But the second part was of no interest to me yet, as it would be a few months before it was finished.

So, taking my place on the roster, I contented myself with electric work, resigning myself to the fact that this was going to be my depot for the rest of my railway career. My grade was now a motorman, meaning I could only transfer to another electric depot as a motorman, but there was not another depot to equal Victoria Eastern in my opinion. There was plenty of running work, the one early turn being 04.50 for the 05.10 to Sheerness and the latest turn being the 23.10 from Dover Priory arriving at Victoria at 00.35. Coupled to the fact that there was a good crew of drivers to work with, I was quite happy to accept what I considered to be a prime position. Only one thing spoilt it for me, something that I tried so hard to put out of my mind, but each time I crossed that bridge over Queens Road station there it was, one of those machines waiting to go to Waterloo with smoke rolling down the smokebox, or chasing off down to the west country, or returning tender empty of coal with that white haze around the chimney. I would think, 'That fire is right for running into Waterloo, light and bright.' But all this had to be forgotten as I was now a motorman at Victoria.

During the first few months of my service at Victoria a change was made in the Conditions of Service Agreements, a change that was to affect me immensely. Possibly I had brainwashed myself into accepting what I now had: a new job, new timing and a new railway. But one of the changes written into the new agreement was that the grade of motorman was to be abolished and all motive power drivers would now be designated 'driver' for promotion and redundancy, regardless of what form of traction was involved. The meaning of this change eluded me at the time.

My life was now revolving around stopping trains to Orpington, Sevenoaks and Sheerness, main liners to Ramsgate and Dover and boat trains to Dover Marine. The boat trains were everyone's favourite, a fast run over the seventy-odd miles to the coast and then two, three or even four hours before the return journey, in the summer time to stretch out on the beach or even take a fishing rod and catch pout whiting from the jetty. Sometimes when the weather was rough the cross-channel boats would have to heave to outside the harbour, and this would mean a wait of anything up to six hours for the return trip.

Folkestone boat trains were still being steam hauled (as the third rail to Folkestone was not yet complete), worked by Bricklayers Arms men.

Having now learned all the roads applicable to Victoria Eastern, plus a few on the Central side for good measure, I was the complete electric driver. Memories of the thrill of riding a fast footplate and pitting myself against an unpredictable steam engine were fast fading. Likewise the talk in the driver's mess room seldom broached the subject of steamers. Were we all now accepting the fact that this was as far as we went? After all, there was nothing else to look forward to. Having one big link, in common with all electric depots, there was no 'next link' to look forward to, no top link to aim at with the accompanying senior work. Perhaps all drivers performing the same duties was the best way, but it only emphasised the fact that we could go no higher, this was it until we all retired. For myself, I had 34 years to do – could I really stick this for that long? Would time condition me to suburban work?

Take a typical suburban duty, six trips between Victoria and Orpington with a forty-minute break between the third and fourth trip: over eighty miles and seventy-eight stops and

43. No. 35009, 'Shaw Savill', under the coal hopper at Nine Elms having run down light engine from Waterloo. She will now be coaled, watered, and have her fire cleaned for the return trip. The fireman is no doubt asking the coalman for some lumps – he always knew which chute contained lumps and which would disgorge rubbish. Having cleaned the fire the fireman will use the lumps to make up a good fire, then call again at the hopper on the way out to top up with whatever coal the coalman decides to give him. Listening to the coal coming into the tender, the fireman would know whether he was getting lumps or small rubbish, but having built a good fire he knew he would cope.

43. John Ashman FRPS

take the full shift to do it. Or all stations between Holborn and Sevenoaks with a stopping train to Wimbledon and back before working to Sevenoaks again. Even the Kent coast trains were all stations from Chatham to Ramsgate or Dover, or semi to Ashford then stopper to Margate via Wye, Chilham and Chartham. Thank goodness we had our boat trains.

It was while working one of these stopping

trains up one night, the 23.10 from Dover, that the realisation came to me. Even though I'd been at Victoria now for nearly three years I wasn't accepting that this was the end of the road. I realised that the agreement made in 1961 could be used by me to transfer to Nine Elms. I still had an accommodation move left, a move in the grade. As we were all drivers, regardless of what form of traction we drove, I could transfer to steam engines again.

For a few days I weighed the pros and cons of such a move. I had a good depot as electric depots go, my colleagues were second to none, and most important I felt that at last I was accepted as a South Eastern man. It was now five years since the country bumpkin from the South Western had, with a little trepidation, made his way over the invisible barrier that divides the two divisions, but I decided that I was going to apply to go back on my 'home' ground.

Having submitted my application on the appropriate form for a move to Nine Elms I now had to wait again for the wheels to turn. As a matter of fact I had to wait another seven months before I heard anything, and during this time I began to think that I had left it too late. The talk was now of the electrification of the Bournemouth road – was I going to miss the boat? The summer of 1964 came and went and with the knowledge that steam depots ran down in work content in the winter I began to despair. Surely a depot the size of the Elms must have some men retiring by now, or had my application been overlooked? Then one Thursday in early October, I signed on from the electric depot at Stewarts Lane, having empties to work to Victoria, and was told to ring the roster office at London Bridge. 'You have to report to Nine Elms next Monday,' said a cold voice at the other end, and that was it, three days' notice. Three days that seemed endless, until Saturday when I left Victoria and some very good friends

44. The valve and piston gear of a rebuilt Bulleid Pacific. This is what I left the kid-glove environment of Victoria for. This picture is typical of the last days of steam, with dirt, oil and steam everywhere. It did not do much for the morale to have to prepare an engine for service in this condition. All pins having only a small degree of movement are fitted with grease nipples, while the small end retains the proven oil reservoir. Note the position of the radius on the combination lever: the radius rod is fixed below the valve spindle, which denotes an inside admission engine.

for the last time.

Driving down Brooklands Road on Monday morning, I noted with a little sadness the devastation all down one side. The last time I had seen this road it had been alive with people, noise, kids and dogs, full of an atmosphere that can only be found in a London street. But at least they had left the old Brooklands Arms standing, a pub that was separate from the Elms and yet so much a part of it.

I reported to Mr Gilchrist, the shedmaster, with a feeling that I had done all this before. I walked alongside the pit roads to make myself known to the foreman and roster clerk. Suddenly, I was part of this great depot. The noise, the smell, the smoke and the activity put all memories of electric traction behind me, and I felt that I had been here all my life. Being no stranger to Nine Elms, I was going to slot into my new job easily.

Having done the necessary reporting, I was given a fortnight to refresh myself with the roads applicable to number two link. I would then take the place in that link of my old friend, Fred Prickett, who was moving up to the top link. Here I was, with very conservative ideas about footplate promotion instilled in me at Bournemouth, barely thirty-four years of age and about to take the place of a man with twice my seniority and experience. It didn't seem right. I only hope I filled the position as well as

the man who was leaving it.

Making my way home that day, I knew that I would have no trouble in adapting myself. Even my lack of steam engine driving experience would not hinder me as I was thrust up near the top of the ladder. Perhaps being a third generation footplateman helped – I suppose something must rub off.

The next day I made my way to Waterloo to refresh my knowledge of the Bournemouth road and, climbing on to the footplate of the 08.30, I made my request as was customary to the driver. He was my old colleague, Reuben Hendicott. We had started cleaning together at Bournemouth and he was also my very first fireman, being on the shovel when I had passed for driving in the practical test. When I left

Bournemouth nearly six years earlier, he had still been a fireman, with slightly less chance than I had of obtaining a driving appointment at that depot. Eventually he had seen the red light and transferred to the metropolis, finding himself in number two link at Nine Elms. Unlike me, though, he had transferred straight to the Elms, where he had been now for just over a year.

During the run down to Bournemouth, I found that I had lost none of my knowledge of the road, despite my six years' absence. I remembered what a driver had said years ago: 'As it unfolds before me so I recognise it.' How true this was.

Watching fireman Stanley perform, I found my palms itching to feel the smooth shaft of the

45. Mike Esau

46. Mike Esau

45. A rebuilt West Country at Woking with the 8.30 am Waterloo–Bournemouth flashing through on the down fast, the driver getting ready to lengthen the stroke of the valves just a little, once clear of the junction, for the steady climb up to milepost 31, then pulling the valves up to a shorter stroke to sweep down towards Sturt Lane. Sheer bliss, and to think we got paid for it as well. The rebuilt on the local looks pretty well up together as this must be the last few months, since already the shield and nameplate have gone. It is remarkably clean, with just a wisp of steam from the blower supply pipe.

46. No. 34077, '603 Squadron', in Nine Elms shed. The cathedral-like atmosphere of an engine shed has really been captured here. Having looked at scenes such as this hundreds of times, even the hardest footplateman would be stirred as he made his way down the lines of these patiently waiting machines to find his own charge for the day. Engines always appeared to stand higher off the ground in the sheds, no doubt an illusion created by the low roof and smoke chutes. All would be surrounded by an indescribable silence, broken only by the gentle simmering of these giants.

shovel again; the joy of mastering the engine was far from dead. However, the fireman was obviously enjoying his job and I didn't have the heart to ask him if 'I could have a go'!

Arriving at Bournemouth, I made my way to the depot that held so many memories for me, meeting many men, shed staff, fitters and footplatemen, having to explain over and over again why I was back on home territory. A perusal of the rosters revealed that, had I not left the depot, I would now be off the main line and rostered in the 'old man's' gang as a fireman. I would've been passed and standing about eight from getting a driver's job. As it was, I had been on top rate driver's pay for nearly four years now, so I considered that the move had been beneficial to me.

I left Bournemouth with cynical thoughts that at least I had given them something to talk about. I caught the 12.40 up train with the Bournemouth crew of Driver Samson and Fireman Tabor. Leaving Southampton and making our climb towards the 'safety' of Round-

wood and Litchfield, I thoroughly enjoyed myself giving George Tabor a 'dig' out. Swinging the shovel around the firebox of that Merchant and trimming the injector to match my success, I was more than satisfied to find the art was still there.

On my way home from Waterloo that afternoon with a spring in my step, I felt more like a young cleaner just completing his first firing turn than a candidate for main line driving. I was confident that I had no need to go over the Bournemouth road again, I found that I had forgotten nothing and apart from a couple of colour light distant signals and a colour light up advance at New Milton, nothing had changed. Even the stopping marks for water were firmly imprinted, even though I had not been called upon to perform this delicate operation. I'd watched Joe 'stop right' enough times.

My very first driving turn was down with the 2.45 am paper train to Bournemouth, and at that time return with the 'Royal Wessex'. I did not sleep very well the evening before. I say evening because I went to bed very early on the Sunday: I had long ago learned that the only way to tackle very early turns of duty was early to bed. Years ago, if I was on at 01.50 I would have stopped up all evening and gone straight to work, recouping sleep during the day. But now my social life took a back seat and I preferred to get a good rest before going to work. So as I've said I didn't sleep very well – who would under similar circumstances?

At last the time came and I signed on. The engine was already prepared for us and was standing under the coal hopper. I noted the water running down the back of the tender, showing that she had only recently been topped up from the water column, plenty of coal and the roof swept off, black smoke silently rolling down the side of the smokebox, safety valves not lifting – outwardly a good preparation. All this I noted as I walked past on my way to the drivers' cabin to meet up with my fireman. I was back in my old role of footplateman without any effort.

Entering the cabin I was greeted with the swashbuckling atmosphere that could be found only in an enginemen's messroom at night. Besides the night spare men and pit relief men, there would be men waiting to get home on the all-night bus service, some waiting for the first trains and others who were early turn having to come in on the last services at night. As usual a card school was in progress with many waiting their chance to fill a vacated seat. The atmosphere could only be likened to a saloon bar in a wild west movie, with tea taking the place of beer. But pair these men off and put them on a footplate and the free-for-all leg-pulling would be left behind in the cabin.

Amidst the bedlam I met up with John Chambers, my fireman, and greeted him with the age-old question, 'Have you got your tea-can, son?' He replied that he was fully equipped, and I retorted with 'I hope you've brought your muscles with you. Let's go!'

Having tested the vacuum brake and waited for John to release the hand brake, I opened the regulator and eased her up towards the signal. The pointsman had already phoned the signal box that we were ready and with the signal in the off position I gave her more steam. Pulling out of the Elms without a slip, I was satisfied that the sanders were working. Remembering the poor sanding when last I worked these engines, I brought the engine to a stand behind the signal in the departure road. John remarked that we would have to wait for the 02.15 to go by before the signalman would have us out and up to Waterloo.

As we waited, a low moan from the Pacific working the 02.15 down brought me back to reality. John replied by easing our whistle valve open enough to emit a similar acknowledgement and they were gone. I opened the small vacuum ejector and looked back at the signal: it was off for the up through, so easing the regulator open we were on our way to Waterloo. Following the rolling tender over the crossover points at Loco Junction, I checked the signals at green and pulled the lever up into 40 per cent. This would trundle us along at about the correct speed to prevent large amounts of coal being blown back into our faces. Rounding Vauxhall I closed the regulator and without thinking looked over at John. 'Green up the main,' he yelled: he didn't need to be told the drill, and I hadn't forgotten.

The yellow outside Waterloo was heralded with a blast from the AWS horn: cancelling out, I let her run back towards the home signal. 'Right,' said John, 'number ten road.' It was my turn now to check the two ground signals as we dropped down through the many points and into number ten platform back on to our train. Buffering up to the train (it was a long time since I'd done this), I noticed the 02.30 am paper train to Portsmouth via Eastleigh pulling out, the fireman already darting the fire to get it hot and bright. By now John was down between the tender and the train coupling on, and when he'd finished I created the brake and opened the steam heating valve, noticing that John had gone to the front of the engine to put the head code lights on and taken the hand brush with him, another sign of a good fireman. I'll bet he checked that the smokebox door was tight as the fireman who had prepared the engine could have forgotten to tighten it: a loose smokebox door would not only result in a poor steaming engine, but also be very dangerous for the crew.

Shrill whistles echoing up the platform from the station staff brought me back to reality, back to the fact that I was once again on the main line,

47. Five different classes lined up towards the end of steam at Nine Elms. As this drew ever closer many engines found their way across to the site of the old Nine Elms shed and were left to await the last, lifeless journey to the scrapyard. Once they were dumped over here, they were never put into steam again. The two 'U' class 2–6–0s nearest the camera have found their way across from the South Eastern side, to judge by the warning signs for the overhead wires. Visible here are the massive smoke shields of the rebuilt Pacific, to capture the wind at speed and drive the exhaust from the squat chimney up and away from the driver's vision (in practice this did not always work).

but this time on the other side of the footplate. Picking out the green 'right away' signal from amongst the many lights that formed the back-cloth to my view of Waterloo, I checked the starting signal, green with the large 'M' in the route indicator. Giving the engine steam, I watched the steam chest gauge rise in response to the regulator, felt the footplate move as she took steam on one side and moved her load. Waiting a few beats for the steam chests to blow out any water, I closed the cylinder cocks, gave her more steam and silently revelled in that wonderful moment as the engine thrust her way across the points and out on to the down main. As I shortened the stroke of the valves, I realised that every move to bring the best out of this machine that I now captained would come naturally. The many times that I had left Waterloo with Joe, waiting and watching his next move, working the fire and boiler to his demands, had been the best training I could ever have had. I suspect that all drivers were influenced by the drivers that they had fired to on the main line, with perhaps a few ideas of their own added.

As we steamed under Loco Junction signal

79

48. No. 35012, 'United States Line', easing down for the cross-out on to the up main at St Denys Junction. Had the train been routed up the main from Northam Junction, half a mile back, it would have been much more beneficial to the crew as they could keep momentum going as they started to climb the bank. Time would be lost here as the crossover was negotiated, and the engine would have to be worked that much harder. The siting of this signal was one of the most misleading on the South Western. If the post had been positioned between the two up roads it would have been self-explanatory. As it was, more than one engine had finished up on the sand drag on the up platform of St Denys.

48. Mike Esau

box with the reverser at 20 per cent cut–off, the injector singing away, I was already preparing for the next move, that of shutting off by the carriage washer and bringing the train down to 40 mph for Clapham Junction curve. As we approached the washer with the engine just starting to get into her stride, it struck me how close Clapham Junction seemed to be at night. Shutting off steam and preparing to bring the speed down, I noted John shutting off the injector, easing the blower on and half opening the fire door – this lad knew his routine.

As we entered the curve through Clapham, I made sure the brakes were fully released and opened her up again. Giving the customary glance over the footplate, I just caught the water disappearing up into the top nut as it was lifted by the regulator, and John giving the steam gauge a satisfied glance as he closed the fire door and shut off the blower. I remember only too well how good it felt to come out of Clapham curve with a full head of steam and a boiler full of water. Coming out of Clapham 'right' determined how good a trip it was going to be. If things weren't just right at this point, you could be working hard for every ounce of steam for the

80

rest of the journey.

The trip to Bournemouth was now a matter of routine, a routine learned from Joe. I found that over the miles and station stops, I was using the same shut-off points, waiting for the roll and kick of the footplate in the same places, stopping right for water at Southampton and expecting and getting from John the tip for those signals that he saw first, with complete disregard for the fact that this was the first time that I had ever worked a main line train as a driver. The six years that I had been away from the Bournemouth road were completely forgotten.

Arriving at Bournemouth, we made our way across to the steam depot and the drivers' cabin to have our break. We had nearly three hours before working the return trip with the 'Royal Wessex' at 08.40, nearly three hours in the gloomy interior of Bournemouth cabin, though I did notice a few alterations due no doubt to the Railways and Factories Act. There used to be a great big open grate capable of holding two hundredweight of coal and an old cast-iron boiler complete with tap mounted alongside that must have been there since the depot was built about a hundred years previously. All this had now been taken out and bricked up and a large slow combustion stove stood starkly out from the wall. The hours that had been spent in front of that open fire talking steam engines by generations of footplate men through the years, the warmth and atmosphere keeping more than one from his bed. The countless gallons of water that had been drawn off to wash off the oil, coal and grime, drawn off into buckets that were encrusted with a hard skin of oil and coal. Nobody ever thought of cleaning these buckets, it was all an accepted part of the job. In its place there was now piped hot water to three sinks. I suppose altogether it was an improvement, but the character of the drivers' cabin that had remained unaltered for all those years had now gone.

My former driver, Joe, signed on at 06.00 on light duties. He told me that he had had enough of the main line, and as he now had only a few months to do before retirement, he had opted to come off the main line and perform engine duties in the shed. What a waste of a good engineman, but believe it or not, some drivers did get fed up with it, though I believe that a lot of it was to do with the fireman they had. Joe was not an aggressive man and if he had a fireman who took advantage of him, this is just the sort of thing he would do. I know that when I fired to him, it was a pleasure to come to work, and I respected him as the boss.

Presently it was time to make our way to Bournemouth up platform. After a good break we were both anxious to get on with it and get home. John had filled the tea-can with cold water and it would be replenished at Southampton. He was going to need it more than I, as the 'Wessex' was one of the hardest trains to work and time – at least it had been when last I'd worked it as a fireman and I had no reason to suspect otherwise. I remembered when I used to get the 'Wessex' ready – Bournemouth top link used to work it then – and heaven and earth was moved to keep the best Merchant Navy at the depot on this duty. How their faces would fall if we ran in with a West Country.

Today we had a rebuilt West Country and, letting her feel her feet out of Bournemouth and up past the goods yard with plenty of lever for the incline, I could feel this engine was 'up together'. A crisp, even, exhaust note, each one separate from the next, denoted the valves were in perfect time and valve and piston rings tight. No more than the normal waste of steam from the front end; this engine was a good one. With over 430 tons behind and the timings of this train, she had to be good.

As we pounded past Goods Junction signal box, I started pulling the lever up, knowing that by the time we were going through Pokesdown she would be in her stride for the run down Christchurch bank, preparing for the assault on Hinton bank. John had had a comfortable trip down with the 02.45, but now he was going to earn his mileage. The way he was flashing the shovel in and out he didn't need reminding, but he wasn't going to get much respite until we reached Worting Junction.

Up through Hinton Admiral and the cutting through the pine trees; what a wonderful setting this was with the exhaust note echoing from the trees. Nothing had altered in the last six years, the characteristics of the road were still there. Everything went all right at Southampton and with John holding the water bag in, I nipped round the motion, feeling the bearings for any sign of running hot, not forgetting to refill his tea-can with fresh water.

The climb from Southampton to Winchester was next, hoping as we approached Eastleigh that the road would be set with all distants off. Then the hard pull to get away from Winchester till finally we rounded the top of the bank and I was able to ease her down for the run to Worting Junction. John had kept the box full and was drawing a bucket of water for a wash up. The worst was now over and, shutting the tender coal-hole, he washed the footplate down, knowing that from here on in he could take it easy. Over Worting flyover and thunder down through Basingstoke, this was the part that everyone enjoyed, that wonderful fast run in, hang on round Farnborough and give her a little more steam at the aqueduct for the slight rise up to Pirbright, easing her again on the open towards Brookwood, peering under the signal gantries approaching Woking for the first glimpse of the distant colour light. Green all the way and through the platform with John hanging on the whistle wire. With everything going

well, she would now be set right until we reached New Malden and the 60 mph limit inside the London area. Passing Hampton Court Junction, John pulled the pricker through the fire to level it off, and to make sure we didn't have too much in the firebox for Waterloo. I could always drop the lever over a bit for the last few miles to shift it, till finally I shut off to bring the speed down for the 60 mph limit.

Giving her just enough steam to maintain this speed, we were soon running smoothly through Wimbledon, with the exception of the rough ride over the points outside Wimbledon box, and through Earlsfield to shut off again for the 40 mph through Clapham Junction. Swinging around Clapham curve, it was only a brief punt up to Loco Junction and Vauxhall. 'One yellow up the relief,' I shouted across to John as I caught sight of the up starter. Dragging the brake slightly, I waited for the call from John as we diverted to the relief road, knowing that the first sight of the next signal would be red, but wait a couple of seconds for the engine to hit the track, and it would turn to yellow or green accordingly. Watching him for his tip, I could see that he'd seen the red then just as quick, 'Green,' he yelled, as he flung out his left arm. I couldn't teach this boy anything.

Blowing the brake off, we rolled around the curve and down into number 13 platform. Getting relief, I said goodbye to John, with a 'See you tomorrow' and made my way across the concourse to head for Streatham, the marching music from the loudspeakers in deep contrast to the noise and sounds that had filled my head for over two hours. Sitting in the peace and quiet of the suburban train, making out my ticket, I suddenly realised how tired I was. Tired but happy, with my first day as a main line driver behind me.

82

7
Final Fling

After a few weeks I lost John as he progressed up to number one link and a young Scotsman named George Bell took his place. At this time about a dozen natives of Glasgow were tempted to transfer to Nine Elms. Most of these had done very little work on steam engines; George had in fact spent most of his service on the diesel shunters at Polmadie and the very first turn we had together was the 02.45 down and back 'Wessex'. He told me that he had a little experience on Standards but nothing on Pacifics, and as it turned out we had a Standard down with the 02.45. I could tell he was reasonably at home on these engines and what he lacked in experience he made up in effort; he would soon learn. I nursed the engine for his benefit as much as possible, but these Standards wouldn't run like Pacifics. If you shut off steam on one of these, even down hill, they would lose speed. This was the first time George had been beyond Clapham so he didn't know what he was in for, but he knew enough, probably through listening to other firemen talking in the cabin, to know that he was expected to shovel more coal than he had ever shovelled in his life. But he was a grafter and it was only at New Milton that I had to interfere and tell him that he had enough in there for Bournemouth.

We had a converted West Country on the return trip and again with much sweat George was able to provide the necessary. I told him to stack it under the door and in the back corners and the blast would do the rest. I remember asking George, as we pounded away from Winchester, 'What do you think of the main line now, George?'

His reply was a gem: 'It's nae so bad, Jum, but I preferrr a wee Stundud.'

After a few more weeks I was booked to attend the training school for Warship diesel instruction. For the first week we wrote hundreds of words on the faults and failures of these diesels. As yet I had not been in the cab of a Warship, and in my opinion the first week should have been spent on the engine out on the road. I would then have had an idea of what this machine looked like instead of having to visualise it. It reminded me of when I was being trained as a Royal Navy stoker: we had to draw explicit diagrams of the Admiralty three-drum boiler, turbines, condensers and evaporators, but when I eventually got into the boiler room on the cruiser, *Belfast*, I was lost. It didn't look a bit like I had drawn in my books. This was going to be the case with the Warship course, because towards the end of the second week we were taken round one of these engines and sure enough I felt that I had wasted my time for more

83

than a week. During the third week back in the school everything then started to fall into place, because now I knew what the thing looked like. The last day was spent passing the inspector on our knowledge and ability to handle the engine. Having passed satisfactorily, we now had a further week on the steam heat boilers.

Needless to say, I was more than glad when the fourth week came to an end and I could resume my role at Nine Elms. I was now working the Warships to Salisbury and back, both passenger and freight. Quite honestly I enjoyed working these diesels, and apart from once when the transmission overheated on the leading engine and filled the driving cab with smoke, which meant changing to a steam engine at Basingstoke, I had no trouble with them.

So the happy months at Nine Elms went by, through the summer of 1965 during which time I lost George as he progressed up to the top link, and I gained Mick Peace, 'Young Mick'. He hadn't even started to shave and still looked like an overfed schoolboy, but his heart and soul were in his job with a keenness that far outweighed his youth.

At about this time I became friendly with Howard and John Mills, twin brothers who lived a short distance from me in Streatham. They brought home to me the fact that engine spotting, as we had called it, had got beyond the 'little boy with a notebook' stage. Their enthusiasm was boundless; when it came to classes of engines, they would lose me. Like most other footplatemen the only classes that I knew were

49. The view looking out of the sheds from the drivers' lobby. Driver Johnny Walker is studying the late notices and driver Roy Lovell is walking towards a Brush diesel. The walkways are not, as they look, cobbled, but smooth concrete, covered in a hard layer of oil and dirt. Years before there was one man to keep the whole shed, including the pits, clean — and clean they always were. When I started cleaning there were doors at the end of the shed and, although I never saw them closed, I have heard talk of when in fact the engines were 'shut up' for the night.

49. Mike Esau

50. 'Oy! What you doing up there then!' 'I'm doing my best not to look guilty as I watch for the right away from the platform staff.' But one Mr Mills (see page 84) knew what he was doing 'up there'. The pirates have not been at work on this engine yet, as the nameplate and badge are still evident, or perhaps they are welded on. A tip for anyone having to oil up one of these engines – look from the cab down through the hole where the reverser shaft disappears through the framing, and with the engine moving slowly, when the big end cork becomes visible through the hole the engine is then stopped and is stood right for oiling all points.

those I was directly involved with. The three of us would spend hours talking steam engines and their supply of transparencies was endless. I now found myself noticing the same faces around Waterloo in the early hours wherever there was a steam engine, always at a discreet distance and quite content just to stand and savour the atmosphere that surrounded the engine. And as I got to know more of them I realised that there was a growing band of steam-engine enthusiasts far greater than had been known before.

The winter of 1965–6 brought a new dimension to steam engine driving, something I had never had time to notice as a fireman: that of driving an engine on a crisp frosty morning when the fire seemed hotter, scorching my right leg, with the countryside covered by a blanket of white frost or snow and a stillness in the air that would hold the exhaust from the chimney as a white plume stretching back as far as the eye could see. Topping the incline at Pirbright junction and looking back towards Brookwood was a prime example. The light from the train reflected back on to the coaches as they glided along under the suspended exhaust. Then suddenly hitting a covering of snow in a cutting,

when the noise of the motion and wheels would cease as the snow absorbed all sound but for the snap of the exhaust from the chimney. Confined in the warmth of a Pacific cab, we were more than ever in a world of our own. Sadly the feeling wasn't the same on a Standard, as I would be too busy trying to keep my feet warm. A Standard was the draughtiest engine ever built.

In the spring of 1966, I was booked to attend the Southampton school for Crompton diesel instruction along with Bert Hooker and Dicky Budd. It was during this time that I really got to know Bert. Travelling up and down every day, our conversation revolved around steam engines and birds (two wonderful subjects), but mainly steam engines. Bert's knowledge far exceeded mine and it was only now that I learned that he was directly involved with the inter-region steam trials. How I envied him; how I would have jumped at the chance to show other railways what our Pacifics could do, what firing to a real engine was all about.

I confided to Bert that I only had one ambition left now on the railway, that was to reach the top link at Nine Elms. We all knew that our days on steam engines were coming to an end. Dare I

85

wish that they would last long enough for me to climb that final rung of the ladder that twenty years ago, when I was at Bournemouth and perched on the bottom rung, seemed to stretch a hundred years in front of me? Now here I was within touching distance of the top. Bert told me that his one remaining ambition was to drive the last steam train out of Waterloo. Neither of us knew what was in store for us but it was nice to learn that I wasn't the only one who had secret wishes.

The summer of 1966 started with number two link losing the 'Royal Wessex' on the return trip of the 02.45. Instead we now worked the 07.07 off Bournemouth. Apart from that there was very little difference; we still had the 'Bournemouth Belle' down and back on Sundays, all the Warship work on the Salisbury road entwined around Waterloo shunter, Bournemouth,

51. My first experience with diesel engines was on the now late Warship class. I must admit I enjoyed hammering these engines up and down the Salisbury road. With the Maybach automatic transmission, life was never boring, since each gear change from both ends had to be watched on a series of lights – as a matter of fact there was so much watching to do, I do not think the designer knew we also had to watch out for signals. Once when working away from Woking on the down road I had a 'dust-up' with a Pacific working on the down local. Admitted the local train only had eight bogies on as to my ten, but whereas I had the Warship in notch seven, and had to wait for the engine to 'help herself', the Pacific driver still had much in reserve, and as we raced cab to cab, grinning at each other, he increased the stroke of the valves and pulled away. I did not catch him until he shut off steam for Farnborough. In this picture D800, 'Sir Brian Robertson', is in Clapham cutting with the 6.15 am from Exeter on 4 June 1966.

WINTHROP

SURBITON

52. No. 34009, 'Lyme Regis', passing through Surbiton with 'The Cunarder' Waterloo–Southampton boat train. The driver has Hampton Court Junction in his sights and has shut off steam because, as would happen all too often with a smart run out of Waterloo, the distant signal for Hampton Court is at caution. As the engine swept round the curve into Surbiton a good fireman could catch a quick glimpse of the distant signal under the station footbridge. With a fast engine these seconds would be precious as with a shout of 'On, mate' the anchors would be put on. Then there would be that seemingly endless pause, as the world continued to flash past the cab window until eventually the train would 'dig its heels in'.

Southampton boat trains and 'as ordered' turns when anything could fall your way. All together it was a varied amount of work.

All around us, though, were the signs of electrification. Colour light signal posts were springing up everywhere, insulating pots and lengths of conductor rail were being strung out alongside the running rails. Re-laying of the track started with the ultimate re-timing of trains. Times that had not altered for years now went haywire; many trains were re-routed via the Alton road. At Nine Elms the air of a depot near the end was slowly becoming evident. We all seemed to be going about our business the same as before but one could detect a stillness where once there had been so much activity. Even the Brooklands Arms that now stood so forlornly alone outside the main gate took on an air of despair. Looking in for a 'quick one' to wash down the dust of a day's work it was now possible to walk straight up to the bar instead of having to push through a sea of shiny-topped hats and black serge jackets. I remember once talking to one of the regulars and he said, 'I've been coming in here for over fifty years, I've never worked on the railway and never been inside Nine Elms depot, but I reckon I could drive a train to Bournemouth and back tomorrow.' He'd listened to so much footplate talk over those fifty years and had probably seen every driver on the South Western division at some time or another. Another regular was an old lady who told me that her grandmother used to collect watercress for the markets on the land that Nine Elms occupied. Remember that depots were built where they could get their own supply of water, and Nine Elms still had the

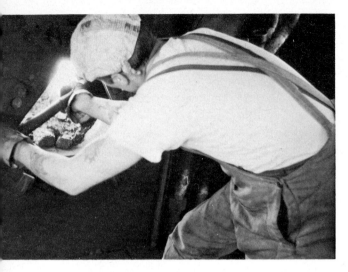

53. Brian Masters, my fireman when in the top link at Nine Elms, delivering some where it mattered most on the Pacifics, in the back corners. During our months together this would be my view of him as he fed that ever-hungry firebox. I did not like the use of gloves as many firemen did: I found that my palms could not 'feel' the shovel, and that my hands got sore around the areas of the seams at the base of the thumbs. Also I did not advise bare arms when firing. Everything on that boiler front was hot enough to burn the flesh severely on the slightest contact. A slip and a fall could cause serious injury.

old pump house.

As the weeds started to grow between the tracks in the old part of the Elms, and more engines were moved over there to rust away, the loss of steam work started to take effect. Not the main line work, but all the little duties that were so much of a big depot were being eroded. This caused the closing up of the links, reducing the number of links but making each link bigger. The top link was going to be increased by twelve; was I going to get my wish and get into the top link?

When the new link structures were revealed I found that I had missed the top spot by one – I would be the next one to go up and was going to have to wait a few more weeks. But sure enough, everything comes to those that wait. Driver Harry Pope, who was close to retirement, decided that he'd had enough of main line work and opted to come off and take a position in the bottom link. I couldn't believe my luck. This was the ultimate. Could I honestly wish for more? August 1966 and I was not thirty-six until September, so at thirty-five years of age I was the youngest ever to get into the top link at Nine Elms.

What a pity it was due for closure – assuming retirement at sixty-five, I could have had thirty years in the top link. I was joining drivers who were driving up and down the Bournemouth road when I was a coaling boy, nearly twenty years ago. George Holloway, a real cockney character whose family so embraced the railway they could practically run it themselves, lost no time in pointing out to me, 'You used to get our bleeding coal down and now you've caught me up!' But what a good innings George had behind him.

My fireman was Brian Masters, who is now driving at Waterloo. He was a big strapping lad, with the eagerness and confidence that was so evident in the Nine Elms firemen. But they were given the chance to prove themselves, whereas at Bournemouth at their age we were never given the chance, our date of birth taking preference over our capabilities. Brian made the job easy, being able to keep one step ahead of the engine requirements, a knack that many firemen didn't have. All the same, more than once, as he will admit, I had to pick up the shovel to help him out. This would give me great delight and I would pull his leg about his abilities, but all in all we worked as a very happy team.

After a while, through realising that Brian was in the unfortunate position of being denied the chance to become a steam driver in the future,

54. My run on no. 35007 on 17 June 1967. Here we are braking heavily through St Denys with the distant signal for Mount Pleasant at caution. I know how a driver feels, having completed the fastest run on the trip, to come up against a signal check. It can be seen how short of rolling stock the South Western were, as there are several different types of coaches in this train. Most of the stock of the South Western were being put through shops ready for the electrification, and trains were made up of anything that had wheels.

we would split the work up. I would do the firing from Waterloo to Worting Junction on the down trips and from Southampton to Worting on the up road. I say it was to give Brian the chance to handle a steam engine, but to be honest, I got great delight out of firing to the engine. That is why I used to pick these parts of the journey where the engine was under load for long periods. It gave one a great sense of satisfaction to keep the steam needle over against the

injector for mile after mile.

Now and again we would be split to cover different duties and I would have other drivers' firemen booked with me. While we were waiting to get away from Waterloo, I would take a piece of chalk from my pocket and deliberately mark forty-five degrees on the cut-off scale. I could practically feel the fireman's thoughts: 'Blimey, is he going to work her there?' though perhaps with much stronger adjectives. Needless to say, I didn't – I never really had any cause to.

The best fireman I ever had fire for me? Well, he was a chap called John Roscoe. I worked a Southampton boat train with him one day and I never saw a finer performance of our 'art'. These were never hard trains to work, either up or down, but the way this fireman performed on this day opened my ever-critical eyes. For instance, while we were at full stretch on the run down to the Docks, between Hersham and Walton-on-Thames, I noticed the boiler was slowly making more steam than we were using, even with the injector working. You would usually accept this and ignore it until she eventually lifted her safety valves and blew the surplus away. Black mark! By the time she'd finished her antics, water would be lost from the boiler,

and water was very precious stuff. Or you could capitalise on your good luck and increase the injector input to get more water into the boiler until she started to drop back in steam, then re-adjust the injector to the right setting again. Very good, red mark! But this boy was after gold. He had noticed she was making steam, but he wasn't going to mess up his injector setting which was just right; he was adjusting the inflow of air through the dampers by closing the dam-

55. No. 35028, 'Clan Line', running into Bournemouth Central, passing the old loco shed. The alterations to the running roads have been completed: the up and down through roads have now become sidings, while the up road runs part of the way on the site of the old sidings, and the new signalling is now in operation ready for the July deadline. One of the Brush diesel locos used to fill in the lack of suitable steam engines, stands in number two sidings. The electric crane used for lifting engines can be seen high above the loco depot's roof.

pers down half a turn on the wheel at a time. In other words, he was using a fine adjustment of the dampers to control the steam pressure and therefore the amount of coal being burned. The fact that he was so coolly controlling every element that the machine needed to give it life, coal, water, air and human muscle, greatly impressed me. I never had the luck to have him booked with me again.

The latter end of 1966 brought Brush engines to Nine Elms duties. The old steam engines were now starting to show signs of wear and tear and the running down of the fitting staff at Nine Elms was very noticeable, so as soon as an engine developed faults, making her unfit for running duties, she would be shoved back into the dark interior of the shed. There was no staff now to sole and heel them, so the Brush diesel was brought into use. For my part, this meant having to spend a week learning these engines, another week away from steam engines. But what an engine the Brush turned out to be; the power from those twin Sulzers has to be experienced to be believed, and the smoothness with

56. Everything that belched smoke and steam on those last two days, 8 and 9 July 1967, they were all 'the last one'. This was no doubt the last steam-hauled boat train out of Weymouth on 8 July. Old '23 was on her last lap, and yet by railway standards she was far from old. The third rail was now laid and together with the new stock, which had slowly increased in various sidings, everything was ready for the big changeover in two days' time. With all those bodies around I hope the driver stopped right for water.

56. Joma Enterprises

which that power comes in is fantastic. And at last it looked as if someone had designed an engine cab without forgetting that a man had to work in it.

Through the winter of 1966-7 all was chaotic on the Bournemouth road. Every trip was marred with re-laying, re-routing and single-line working. I began to forget what a good run down and back was like. The third rail was already creeping its way down towards Bournemouth. Colour light signals were being put up everywhere, notices had to be read carefully as signals and tracks were altered. Train timing ceased to exist, it was a case of get there when you can. But the engines we had left held together pretty well, considering the way they were hammered around the Alton road. I never ceased to wonder how some of the engines reached Southampton going down without running out of water, though rumours were heard of engines running into Southampton and reaching the water column with empty tenders.

I was caught out once on the return trip to Waterloo. I'd filled up at Southampton and then got held at Wallers Ash for an hour. All the time water was being used and, getting away at last, I was turning over in my mind whether to stop at Basingstoke for water or not. Getting the road right through Basingstoke, I found I still had water in the tap, so with no more hold-ups we would be all right for Waterloo. There was a column on Walton-on-Thames up through, the last before London, and getting greens all through Woking, I gave her her head. Everything pointed to a clear run in. But passing Byfleet junction, the repeater distant for Weybridge was at caution and we crept through Weybridge and round towards Oatlands, again being checked at every signal. That was enough to put the water at a dangerous level. Given the road, we would have been scuttling through Wimble-don by now. So I pulled up alongside the column at Walton-on-Thames only to find, typically, there was no water. Sending Brian to the signal box with our troubles, I dropped the pricker into the tender and found we were down to six inches – I'd never been so low in water. Brian came back with the news that the only water at Walton was in the yard, and they had trouble with signalling through Surbiton. The only thing for it was to get unhooked and get back in that yard double quick. Taking on half a tender of water, we returned to the train and, with a much easier mind, resumed our journey.

By now the Cromptons were in use, electric units were undergoing tests and, with a certain amount of sadness, we prepared for the last few weeks of steam. But what a few weeks they were; sales of film and tape rocketed and didn't we have a good time? Engines were called upon to give of their very best and a bit more and they responded well. They seemed determined to go out in a blaze of glory, management turned a blind eye to the early arrival of trains and even Weston to Farnborough in 14 minutes with 514 tons didn't bring any comment, although I expect a few eyebrows were raised behind the scenes. The engineering work was all but finished in preparation for 7 July, quite a few records were made and broken, and it was a time that will be remembered not only by the few footplatemen that were left but also by the many enthusiasts who seemed to be everywhere at all times of the day and night. The increase in ticket sales must have paid for all the extra coal that was burned.

My last fling was the 08.30 down on Saturday 17 June 1967. For the following three weeks I was going to be on another course. The last three weeks of steam, just my luck! However, having a good engine, 35007, I was tempted to give her her head and let her go. I'll admit to burning much more coal than was necessary but Brian,

57. Sunday 9 July 1967, and driver Ray Hardy of Bournemouth at the controls of no. 35030 on the 2.07 pm Weymouth–Waterloo, the last steam run to Waterloo. I was surprised how the management turned a blind eye to the activities of both employees and enthusiasts over the last few days, or were they too pre-occupied with getting their new service out on Monday 10 July 1967? And there were quite a few footplatemen who made their way to the stations to witness the last rites, though not many would admit it. I relieved Ray at Waterloo, along with the many diehards who did not want to go home, and dear old '30 paid her last respects to Waterloo.

57. Joma Enterprises

knowing this was the end, shovelled it in without complaining as I tried to shift it straight out of the chimney. For years I'd religiously and economically worked engines but this time the temptation was too great. I wanted to hear the engine work as I'd never heard before, and didn't she respond wonderfully. I only hope all those microphones hanging out of the train windows captured the thrill of that big Pacific being called upon to give more than her best. Getting off the footplate at Bournemouth for the last time I could feel the heat from the steam chest, smell the oil that was practically boiling around the front end and suddenly all was peace and quiet after over two hours of beautiful bedlam.

We worked the 12.30 return to Waterloo that day with a Brush. The smooth elegant power of the Brush was in deep contrast to the down trip, as she effortlessly gave me the power that I needed. As Brian and I changed seats at Southampton, as we had done so many times before, we both realised that this was the end of a good team, but it had been good and as we sped towards Waterloo with the soft roar of the twin Sulzers behind us we accepted the fact this was the end.

Having the next three weeks to spend on a course was sheer murder with the last three weeks of steam on the Southern, and here was I stuck in a classroom. Still, it had to be done. My next and last duty at Nine Elms was on Sunday 6 July 1967. I had to relieve on a Warship and prepare her for the 19.00 to Salisbury, then relieve on a Brush on the last Weymouth up. My fireman was John Cotty and as we waited we, and the last few enthusiasts who seemed reluctant to give up, heard the sound of a Pacific and into number 11 platform rolled 35030. It seemed that the Brush had failed and here was the very last steam engine into Waterloo. We were going to have to work her back to the Elms to throw the fire and life out of her for the last time, and so, what do you know, I worked the last engine out of Waterloo. As we prepared to make our exit, flash bulbs popping, I overheard one enthusiast remark to his friend, 'Well that's it, now we can start chasing girls.'

The Monday following my final escapade with steam I reported at Waterloo. I still had three days' training to do on the REPs (Restaurant Electro-Pneumatics) so this gave me plenty of time to get accustomed to my new job. I think we were all a little bit bewildered, having to get used to new duty numbers, new trains, new signing-on times and new accommodation. There would be no more searching the shed for tools in the early hours of the morning, no more clambering over and inside a steam engine while clutching a lighted flare lamp and full feeder in one oily hand. No more wedging oneself up behind the inside big end to oil the main bearing, reaching across the top of the web to get to the eccentric strap oil wells, all the time listening for signs that the engine might move; hoping that the engine just moving behind would stop short, after he's filled the pit with steam and blown the flare lamp out. Or squeezing up alongside the inside small end only to find that the corks have been pushed in flush, having to balance the feeder and flare lamp on any adjacent part while you grope into your pockets for a penknife and new corks. No more wet shirts taking water, or hooking the coal dust out that always seemed to collect most behind the ears and inside your collar. No more gulping down a stewed beverage that long ago had ceased to resemble tea. No more would we grab the side of the cab at recognised points as she rolled but having complete faith in her stability as she settled to an even keel once more having not missed a beat. No more at the end of the day gently easing that large accumulation of assorted metals down the bank into Nine Elms.

Saturday, 17 June 1967. Locomotive 35007, 'Aberdeen Commonwealth'. Load 11 for 371 tons. Driver J. Evans. Fireman B. Masters.
Train: 8.30 am Waterloo to Bournemouth.

Distance.		Sched.	Actual	Speeds
0.0	Waterloo	0	0.00	
1.3	Vauxhall		4.11	37
3.9	Clapham Junction		7.41	40
7.2	Wimbledon		11.41	60
9.7	New Malden		14.04	68
12.1	Surbiton		16.01	71
13.3	Hampton Court Junction		17.05	75
17.1	Walton		20.10	72
19.1	Weybridge		21.56	72
21.6	West Byfleet		24.10	71
24.3	Woking		26.26	68
28.0	Brookwood		29.36	70
31.0	Milepost 31		32.14	69
33.2	Farnborough		34.02	75
36.5	Fleet		36.36	80
39.8	Winchfield		39.03	80
42.2	Hook		41.29	27 per. way.
47.8	Basingstoke		48.41	38 signals.
50.3	Worting Junction		52.53	35 signals.
52.5	Wooton		56.10	50
56.2	Roundwood		59.43	68
58.1	Micheldever		61.13	80
61.8	Wallers Ash		63.43	95
66.6	WINCHESTER CITY	71½	67.50	——
3.1	Shawford		5.10	51 p/w. sigs.
6.9	Eastleigh		8.56	60
9.2	Swaythling		11.07	65
10.6	St Denys		12.36	40 signals.
11.6	Northam Junction		14.37	22
12.6	SOUTHAMPTON CENTRAL	19	17.37	——
0.9	Millbrook		3.05	38
3.3	Totton		5.57	54
6.1	Lyndhurst Road		8.53	62
8.9	Beaulieu Road		11.13	75
13.5	Brockenhurst		15.06	68
14.5	Lymington Junction		16.00	66
16.3	Sway		17.38	72
19.3	New Milton		20.00	88
25.0	Christchurch		24.23	65
27.5	Boscombe		26.57	signal stop.
28.7	BOURNEMOUTH CENTRAL	37	32.42	——

With several signal and per. way checks, an additional call at Winchester and a signal stop at Boscombe, the overall running time was only two minutes outside the old 'two-hour' Bournemouth trains. Net times 62 + 16 + 29½ minutes.

58. D6549 pulls out of Andover Junction with nos. 35023 and 35008 in tow to Salisbury in August 1967, a scene that we saw so often. With a certain amount of sadness we watched these fine machines formed into what can only be described as a wake, as with side rods and valve gear removed they were slowly dragged to the end of their road. Andover signal box does not look all that healthy either. Having engines of ever-increasing sizes thunder past, only inches away, for years on end has certainly played havoc with the foundations. And by the look of the exhaust from the diesel, she is doing her best to emulate a Pacific getting stuck into the bottom of Grateley bank.

58. Joma Enterprises

All this was now behind us and I was secretly amazed how smoothly the change-over to electrification went. Not only with the trains but with the men, everything fell into place the first time. The thought and organisation that went into this venture, a complete change-over in virtually one day, was terrific. The constant high running speed that was required to time the hundred-minute service was quite surprising. Instead of jogging up to the bank from Eastleigh to Litchfield at a steady forty-five to fifty, as we had been used to, we now rose to the height of St Paul's Cathedral as if the bank wasn't there.

On 4 September, along with my old colleague Reuben Hendicott, I was transferred to Bournemouth. So here I was back home via Stewarts Lane, Victoria, Nine Elms and Waterloo and my fifth depot as a driver. The good old Lane I must remember as my first depot as a driver, when I was lifted from one side of the footplate and put on the other, a bewildered country bumpkin overawed by the activity and work rate of my new depot. Victoria Eastern, the finest men anywhere, so typical of all Eastern men. Not forgetting the drivers' mess room at Victoria, with the invisible wall down the middle, Eastern men one end and Central men the other: no one would think we worked for the same firm. Then there was the Elms, which had to be my best times on the railway, but it was all over now.

Back in Bournemouth, making sure I kept my back to the wall (old practices die hard), I found that the old attitudes were trying to be retained by certain of the drivers. The days when one man went to London and looked down on the man not permitted to go beyond Brockenhurst, were now out; we were all trained on the same forms of traction and all performed the same work. The days when a man was penalised by his birth date finished with the steam engine.

The Wednesday before Christmas 1967 I moved my household and family back to Bournemouth. As I was on a redundance move all my expenses were paid for by the railway, a big help and gratefully accepted. So with my family now installed I could settle down to a clean and, in my opinion, a good job. Perhaps it is not so exciting as the footplate but none the less it was interesting with the speed that we now run the trains, and the different forms of traction involved. Nobody talks trains and diesels to the extent they used to with the steam engine, and as time goes on we realise that we have lost the character that was so much part of the magic of the footplate. Once, our grades were a bit of a mystery to all but footplatemen; an engine emerged from the bowels of an engine depot and performed her duties witnessed only by the crew who had to make her perform. At the end she was unhooked and with tail lamp in place disappeared back into the engine sheds. The footplate was the sacred domain of the driver and fireman and only they knew what went on. Motive power work was a world apart from the rest of the railway. But now everyone knows what our work consists of, every one has access to the driving cabs and when the train stops at the end of the journey so does our duty. We now have guards and shunters riding as second-men in the cabs of diesels, but in the name of progress we have accepted it.

Now I've got to mention my mate for the last twenty-five years, my wife. She has had to put up with a lot being married to a footplateman, as have all my colleagues' partners. Meals at all times of the day and night, no social life to talk about – how can you when the old man is on at 01.53 in the morning, or 16.59 Sunday afternoon, every other week a late turn with no guarantee that he will walk in the door a few minutes after his day is up. And once there were filthy overalls to wash every week, plus all the other dirty washing that went with the steam engine. Before washing machines it was all hand washed.

I've always thought of my old grandmother, with five men in the family working for the motive power: five lots of overalls to wash and iron, five lots of sandwiches a day to cut and five bottles of cold tea to put up. Besides coping with meals for the different shifts, there was always a

59. Myself on no. 35023 at Southampton with the down relief to the 10.30 am ex Waterloo in September 1966. Having taken water and felt around the bearings for signs of running hot, a practice that I copied from my old Bournemouth drivers, we are waiting for the signals that are still against us. Only once did I find a bearing running hot, and that was a tender bearing. I knocked off the axle-box cover to examine the journal and try to cool it down and get some oil around it. The journal was so hot that it resembled molten glass – you could see right into the metal. The bearing was too far gone and we had to have another engine.

59. R. M. Grainger

meal waiting for somebody on the gas or in the range oven. As a youngster I never had to make a noise about the house as there was always some-one in bed, or getting ready to go or getting up. Besides this she had her usual household chores plus making her own wine, jams and pickles, of which she was a master. Sunday was the time for testing 'Mary's wine', and we could go into the front room, complete with piano and the smell of polish. It didn't matter what time of the day you went into that house, the tea-pot was always hot and there was always an apple tart keeping warm in the range oven. I guess this was just about characteristic of all footplate homes then. Whenever I smell home-made wine now I'm instantly reminded of that house at 93 Campbell Road, Eastleigh, where everything revolved around the steam engine. Even the outside toilet had the weekly notices tied to a nail on the wall.

I've accepted the fact that I am now a train driver, not having much choice, and I no longer walk into Bournemouth mess room feeling my back should be to the wall. And the future? Well, I did find myself reading up on my retirement pension rights the other day. Would I go through it all again? You bet I would. As a fireman I enjoyed every minute of putting life into a steam locomotive and pitting myself against the most unpredictable machines ever invented by man. And as an engine driver, hav-ing control over these machines, well, there are no adjectives strong enough to describe a won-derful experience.

There remains just one loose end to tie up: my grandfather passed away in 1969, being nearly ninety years of age. He had worked on steam engines during the most progressive and excit-ing times of steam transportation, and had then witnessed the decline and final destruction of those dirty, smelly, noisy, magnificent coal con-suming machines of power that were so much of his life and mine.

Index